Extreme
Waterfowl
Hunting

Dedication

This book is a tribute to the women who have made it possible for me to pursue waterfowl to the extreme. To Mom for putting up with Dad and me. To my beautiful wife Laurel for understanding and enduring the passion that drives me. To my "hunting sister" Dawn for showing me that women can be extreme waterfowl hunters, too.

Gratitude.

Bill Miller

Extreme Waterfowl Hunting

Hunter's Information Series®
North American Hunting Club
Minneapolis, Minnesota

Extreme Waterfowl Hunting

Mike Vail
Vice President, Products and Business Development

Bill Miller
Author

Tom Carpenter
Director of Book and New Media Development

Dan Kennedy
Book Production Manager

Heather Koshiol
Book Development Coordinator

Teresa Marrone
Book Design & Production

ISBN 0-58159-003-2

Printed in U.S.A.

1   2   3   4   5   6   7   8   9   10

Contents

North American Hunting Club Executive Director Bill Miller

About The Author

"*I*'ve often asked my mother if somewhere in my upbringing I had a really frightening experience with a web-footed bird. Though she doesn't recollect any such incident, I still figure that some earth-shattering event with a duck must have happened along the way. Why else would I be so driven to hunt ducks and geese wherever they fly?"

So asks the author of *Extreme Waterfowl Hunting*, Bill Miller. And to those who know him well, the question is justifiable. Bill loves (make that lives) to hunt waterfowl.

As the North American Hunting Club's Executive Director, Bill is often asked what his favorite type of hunting is. He hates that question because he never wants to give up any of them, but if he had to make the choice, waterfowl hunting—extreme waterfowl hunting—would win!

Bill's hunting career began more than 30 years ago at age five when his dad carried him on his shoulders to hunt pheasants and ducks on the family farm in eastern Wisconsin. The springer spaniels the Miller family raised were eager hunting companions no matter what the game. Early "solo" hunts were first with a popgun, then a Benjamin pellet gun and finally a 28 gauge Savage Stevens single-shot shotgun. Ducks and better ways to get close to them were always on the young hunter's mind. Grade school and high school teachers who got to read English class essays like "How To Call Ducks" and "Wetlands In Trouble" and "Fit For Firing Line—Improving Shotgunning Skills Through Personal Fitness" can attest to that!

Extreme waterfowl hunting is going where you need to go and doing what you need to do to successfully collect ducks and geese. Bill exhibited that manic obsession from his earliest hunts! In fact, the very first time Bill was allowed to carry a gun in the blind, his dad shot a bluewing teal that fell into the bog surrounding the spring-fed lake the pair was hunting. Eager to show that he could do it all, the young hunter leapt from hummock to hummock and actually beat the dog to the bird. He held it high to show his dad back in the boat and promptly broke through the bog mat.

Bill struggled out of the armpit-deep mud and stinking black water, slogged back to the boat, and presented the tiny drake teal to his dad without allowing a feather to be out of place on the trophy. Later that warm opening day afternoon, he took his first shot at a Canada goose while sitting in the boat in his skivvies, with the rest of his clothes hanging on nearby trees and bushes to dry!

Another early, memorable, and certainly extreme duck hunt included dragging his best friend's mom from bed at 3:00 a.m. to drive the young hunters to the local public marsh so they'd have enough time to paddle the canoe and break ice all the way to the blind and set a spread of six dozen decoys by shooting time! Despite shotgunning skills that still needed time to mature, the mallards "were in" and the bag made photos that still grace Bill's hunting albums.

Real glory days of extreme hunting arrived with a driver's license. That same best friend went on to star on the high school football team, so many was the Saturday morning Bill would be banging on that family's front door demanding that Mike get up to go duck hunting, no matter how late he had gotten home from the game the night before! A like-minded extremist, Mike never failed to answer the call.

Even college at the University of Wisconsin–Eau Claire where Bill majored in journalism and environmental communications couldn't stifle the extreme duck hunting passion. Bill plotted his fall semester course selection so he could take off at 2:30 in the morning on Fridays during duck season to drive the four hours home, eat a big breakfast prepared by his grandmother, then be set up in a local slough in time to catch the ducks returning from the morning trip to the fields. Of course he'd hunt Saturday, Sunday morning and drive back to school on Sunday afternoon! Professors who gave quizzes or exams on Monday morning soon understood the addiction of extreme waterfowl hunting.

Right out of school, Bill started with the North American Hunting Club as Associate Editor. That was in 1984 when the NAHC had approximately 75,000 members and *North American Hunter* published just six times per year with fewer than 100 pages per issue. As the NAHC recognizes its 20th Anniversary in 1998, Bill celebrates 14 years with the Club. As Executive Director, he's proud to assist a membership of more than 850,000 avid hunters, and as Editor, oversee the publication of seven issues per year of *North American Hunter,* some as big as 200-plus pages.

Bill also hosts "North American Outdoors", "The Shooting Sports", and "Shoot More, Shoot More Often" on ESPN, as well as the Club's video tape series.

The magazine and the television shows have afforded him the opportunity to hunt waterfowl in more than a dozen states, five Canadian provinces and Mexico. He shoots competitive trap, skeet and sporting clays. He is "on call" to be among the first to evaluate new products and designs from ammunition, firearm and hunting gear manufacturers.

Bill and his unbelievably understanding wife, Laurel, operate Northwings Kennel, which specializes in breeding and raising Labrador retrievers for hunting, field trials and hunt testing, and great family pets.

The drive to go wherever the birds go and do whatever it takes to collect them is stronger in Bill today than ever! Wherever waterfowl of any description migrate across North America, you're likely to find Bill hunting them. As much as the constraints of making a living to support his addiction will allow, Bill Miller is an extreme waterfowl hunter. That's why he was chosen to prepare this book for the North American Hunting Club Hunter's Information Series.

Introduction

Over the years, the North American Hunting Club team charged with selecting books and authors worthy of NAHC members probably came to look on me as a pest. Every time we had a meeting, every time the subject came up in casual conversation at the coffee pot, I was pushing to write a new book for the Club about waterfowl hunting. I was certain that I could share some hard-earned information and hunting tips that would enhance the waterfowl hunting skills, success, enjoyment, safety and ethics of fellow NAHC members whose passion, like mine, is for hunting ducks, geese, swans and cranes.

Finally the time came for a new NAHC waterfowling book. And all the ground work I laid about who should write it paid off.

The team finally said, "Just do it!" I'm not sure if it was a gesture of enthusiastic encouragement or a statement of relief that I wouldn't be bugging them about it anymore!

I sat down at a blank computer screen to finally put down in electronic black and white the outline for a book that's been in progress between my ears for the last 20-plus years! The working title for the book was *Advanced Waterfowl Hunting*. It was to share the advanced tricks and techniques and equipment knowledge spawned by a lifetime pursuit of ducks and geese and meeting like-obsessed hunters across North America.

Then along came the waterfowl hunting season. As might be expected I spent a lot of time hunting that I probably should have spent writing, but then again each sunrise only comes once! Being there in the sloughs and rivers and lakes and fields turned out to be the right choice. During the time the words for this book were being translated into the binary code of 0s and 1s in the guts of the laptop computer I dragged all over North America that fall, I experienced three life-altering waterfowl hunts.

The first was amongst the beloved prairie potholes of North Dakota. It was near the end of the opening week of Nodak's duck season. I was hunting with my good friend "The Crane Man" Ken Toop and some other buddies of his. Our primary target was sand-hill cranes, but we also took geese and ducks from the combination spread we set each morning.

It was the final day of my trip. When we woke a couple hours before shooting time, it was very warm, but the wind was up and lightning was constant in the southwest. The storm was coming fast.

As the first rain hurried my Labs Sadie and Belle through their morning routine, our small group debated the plan. The field we scouted the night before was almost 30 miles away—it might be out of the storm's path completely. On the other hand, we had already enjoyed several days of incredible hunting—maybe the electrical storm was a sign we should sleep in.

If you knew the group personally, you would know there was never really a decision to be made. We went hunting, but because of the conversation, ended up getting to the field pretty late. The storm was not far behind us.

Though we usually hunt together, this morning's plan was to split up. The layout of the winding slough system interspersed with harvested fields and the fact that I would be leaving earlier than the rest to start the long drive home that day made it seem the right strategy. Hurrying to be in position by legal shooting and to find some kind of cover from the advancing storm, I cut too close to the edge of one slough. I caught the cranes' attention, which put them on the wing with a roar louder than the thunder.

I hoped I hadn't ruined the morning's hunt for my friends, but at this point what could I do? So I hurried on to a small grain field rise some distance from the slough. There Belle and I found a rock pile and nestled against it from the windblown rain.

By now it was several minutes into legal shooting, but the clouds made it very dark and the lightning flashed on three sides of us. Belle and I both lay down in the weeds hoping it wouldn't get any closer. The cranes didn't like the lightning either. Each time they'd line out in one direction, the electricity wove a net among the clouds and scared them back the other way.

For an hour, I lay on my back and watched an incredible show. Swarms of the huge prehistoric birds crisscrossed the sky above me. They were from gun barrel height to 300 feet high. Their trilling filled my ears, and much of the calling was so close I could actually feel the vibration of it in the raindrops. Young birds in the flock sounded like dozens of police whistles as they tried to keep tabs on each other. With the oddly shaped birds silhouetted against the lightning and the growing daylight, the scene seemed nothing short of a special effects film about pterodactyls!

When the storm finally blew past and the birds moved on, I realized I had never loaded my gun! It would have been just too easy and I would have missed something I never will experience again.

Belle and I got up, walked down to the edge of the slough and shot a limit of six ducks of six different species. Then we walked around to where our friends were already picking up their spread because they had finished their limits on cranes in that first flurry. Several had fallen in small potholes, so little Belle made her first retrieves on crane that morning—and water retrieves at that!

I was still in a mild state of euphoric shock when the dogs and I pulled into the driveway at home some nine hours later, and I can't for sure say I'm still not as I relive the memory writing this.

The second adventure was cold. Despite having hunted musk ox in the high arctic on Halloween, I'd say the hunt on the Saint Lawrence River between Montreal and Quebec City was colder. It was just before American Thanksgiving and we were hunting from a sinkbox. Yes, that antique form of big water duck hunting is still legal in some parts of Canada, and it was the reason we were there with Siegfried Gagnon of the Quebec Tourism Department and outfitter Andre Plante of Plante Guide Service.

Every minute of that hunt was a unique experience. Despite air temperatures below freezing, the excitement kept me warm. Even in the two-hour predawn ride to the hunting area and to collect and set the sinkbox and spread, I sat in the bow of the boat, nose to the wind like a retriever pup. If my ears were long enough, they would have flopped from under my stocking cap, too.

We sat for as much as 10 hours a day in the small, submerged confines of the steel box waiting for goldeneyes, bluebills or a wayward oldsquaw or scoter to spot our spread. When they did, many would come sizzling in two feet above the water. Following Andre's advice, we'd wait until they were inside the spread with feet forward and

wings back to stand up and shoot. The shots were point blank and the results very final.

At the end of the last day, even with frozen joints that made sure-footedness less than assured when we transferred from the box to the pick-up boat, I was sure I didn't want to go home. Though just a piece of cold, gray welded steel surrounded by hundreds of square kilometers of 32.5 degree water, that sinkbox was a haven, a shrine. It had made it possible for me to be closer to the feathers of flying diving ducks than I'd ever been before. Sinkbox cold and sinkbox close gives new understanding of the whistle from a goldeneye's wings and the color of blue in a bluebill's bill.

The only way to describe the third hunt is to recall one of those movies or books where a mortal is taken from this earth up to the magnificence of heaven. Just as the mortal begins to experience the joy and glory of the other side, a bookkeeping mistake is discovered on St. Peter's scroll. It isn't yet this conscript's appointed time, so he is sent back to earth to live out his life. He's never the same as before the trip because now he knows what heaven is like.

The on-earth equivalent, at least for a waterfowl hunter who spends most of his time "thrashing" for places to hunt and setting his own decoys in waist-deep ooze, is an audience with the kind of hunting that's done on private duck clubs in the Central Valley of California. My chance came this fall on the invitation of friends at Ducks Unlimited, Filson and Winchester.

Ken Hofmann is a long-time California developer and senior owner of the Oakland A's baseball team. Ken is also an avid waterfowl hunter and conservationist. In fact, he bought the most productive rice farm in the Sink Butte area and, with DU's help, turned it back to natural wetlands. The result is Piper's Patch, a haven for wintering waterfowl and a private duck hunting heaven for Ken and his guests.

Something in the way my whole body shook as we loaded in the gas-powered "mule" for the trip to the blind probably tipped off my hunting companions Mike Jordan of Winchester and Ron Stromstad, DU's Western Region Director of Operations, that I was a little excited. They graciously offered me the first shot of the morning. Even though Mike is from southern Illinois's waterfowling hotbed and Ron is a transplanted North Dakotan who has witnessed the waterfowl spectacle of the prairies, they too sensed this morning would be something out of this world!

Despite the excitement there was no rush. We were blessed by a strong wind that would keep the ducks flying all morning.

We hunched in the pit blind and shared stories of other hunts—some shared, some lived vicariously through one another. We marveled over and over again at the number and variety of ducks, geese, shorebirds and raptors. We shared a once-in-a-lifetime communion *inside* the gates of waterfowling heaven.

Then when it was light enough to identify not only sex and species but trophy quality as well, I stood up and shot a pintail drake for the wall. We took sprigs, greenheads and green-winged teal that morning, and a couple of snow geese, too.

No cinnamon teal swung past our hide that day, but it's just as well. Perhaps it was St. Peter's way of saying, "Don't worry boys. You'll be back when your time comes."

It was these three hunts, which came to pass while this book was being written, that made me realize the theme and title *Advanced Waterfowl Hunting* wasn't right. It's too distant, too technical, too objective. A book worthy of NAHC members had to take them along to these places. It had to share what I believe waterfowl hunting is all about.

Until these hunts and until struggling with this book, I could never put that emotion into words, but now the words have come and the emotion even has a name.

Extreme Waterfowl Hunting is about more than collecting a bag limit of birds. It's about the collection of waterfowling experiences.

When my time finally does come for a permanent visit on the good side of the pearly gates, I hope my life earns the epitaph, "He hunted ducks." Extreme waterfowl hunters who happen to see that tombstone will understand.

Best afield,

Bill

Bill Miller
Executive Director
North American Hunting Club

1

What Is Extreme Hunting?

*E*xtreme sports are those that take human ability, endurance, courage and, yes, sanity to the very edge. As popularized by a television event called "The X Games," which developed with the advent of the espn2 cable television network, extreme sports are a search for an adrenaline rush! They include such things as bungee jumping, base jumping (which is parachuting from tall buildings, cliffs and the like), sky-boarding (sky-diving with a snowboard strapped to your feet), downhill mountain biking, street luge (flying down a paved road while laying flat on your back aboard a giant skateboard) and many more "athletic" endeavors that are as spine-tingling and potentially life-threatening as they are physically demanding.

Depending on your personal point of view, the folks who participate in "extreme sports" might be called athletes or lunatics. No one can deny that part of the reason for trying an extreme sport is to feel the rush—the same rush our ancestors felt when they were part of the hunt. Though the participants may not admit it, extreme sports are a modern day attempt to experience the emotions, the panic, the thrills, the lust, the anger, the fear, the release, the climax that are all part of the fight-or-flight response. Extreme sports are a way to, at least momentarily, reclaim the time when humans almost daily trod the fine line of predator and prey.

The rush of, say, plummeting down a mountain slalom course on a bike with no brakes is a natural high experienced by the body and the brain because of the release of adrenaline, epinephrine, endorphins and about a dozen other biochemicals secreted by the human body in times of physical and mental stress. The reason humans were endowed by God with this complex and satisfying chemistry probably wasn't to artificially stimulate it by intentionally risking life and limb in frivolous pursuits. It's more likely that man, the hunter, was blessed with these natural performance enhancers to allow him to successfully take game to feed himself and to flee from all sorts of predators trying to feed themselves!

Okay, enough with trying to get into the head or subconscious of a crazy street luger. How does the extreme principal apply to duck and goose hunting?

Simple.

Extreme waterfowl hunting is taking duck, goose, swan, crane, etc. hunting to the very edge—to the point where it creates the full bouquet of fight-or-flight emotions which participants in the other extreme sports are trying to experience. Call it fanaticism; call it

Yes, that's the author caught in a weak moment. But remember the extreme waterfowl hunter eats, breathes, and sleeps waterfowling.

obsession, but for any hunter so afflicted, a quickened pulse at the mere thought of going waterfowl hunting is an undeniable fact of life. The higher heart rate and faster, deeper breathing are two of the most basic and noticeable fight-or-flight physiological indicators.

The fight-or-flight response is so deeply instinctive and something so many of us want to feel, the actual event, in this case the hunt, doesn't even have to be underway. The simple thought or visualization of it is enough to get us going. It's the reason extreme hunters spend so much time reliving past hunts and planning future adventures. Such is the plight and the glory of being an extreme hunter.

Who Are The Hunters?

In terms of instincts and terms of genetics it's likely that we are all hunters, man and woman alike ... or at least we were. Society has evolved—in some cases for the better, in some for the worse. Inevitably, that evolution toward "civility" has altered the human species through the millennia. Yet underneath it all, the instinct to hunt, to survive, still has to be there in each of us, no matter how deeply it is buried. How could a few million years have erased a habit on which our survival hinged?

As the Executive Director of the North American Hunting Club, I receive many letters from the Club's nearly

You can pick out extreme waterfowlers by the way they dress. They all sport the layered look!

one million members. One of them, some time back, was from a young NAHC member who was working on a paper for his biology class. His request was for any input the Club could give to help him with his paper on the topic: "Is hunting, overall, morally acceptable?"

We hoped the response he was sent answered his question and helped him get an "A" in his class. More than that, it also outlines pretty well who the hunters are and who they are not:

The choice of topic—weighing the moral acceptability of hunting—seems like an odd one for a biology class. If I'm not mistaken, biology is the scientific study of living things. I hope you aren't experiencing the misfortune of dealing with a teacher who abuses the classroom to espouse pseudo-science in support of a bias against hunting.

The morality of any activity cannot be supported nor denied by charts, graphs or any kind of "scientific documentation." Morals are simply what a society, species ... or an individual of a society or species ... considers right or wrong.

To those of us who love hunting, there is no question of its moral acceptability. Asking whether hunting is right is akin to asking whether breathing, eating or sleeping is right. Hunting is so much a part of human make up, that the immoral act would be not to hunt, thus to deny our nature.

If you accept the Bible as your moral compass, there can be little doubt that hunting is a moral act. It's in Genesis, the very first book, that God dictates that man is to have dominion over the animals. The problem with quoting the Bible is then when you're dealing with animal rightists, so few of them place stock in the Bible as truth. They believe only their own self-conceived morality which they try to impose on everyone else.

I don't have any documents or statistics to give you that reveal why hunting is so important to so many humans, is viewed neutrally by most and considered immoral by a pathetic few. My guess is, however, that the desire to hunt is innate; that it's genetic. But physically founded as it is, the desire to hunt is only activated by socialization; that is, by upbringing.

People who grow up in a climate where hunting is accepted and encouraged will be true to their nature and hunt. Those who are neutral on hunting never have the hunting switch "turned on" in their upbringing, but somehow subconsciously recognize the desire is universal and natural—thus moral.

If this idea is correct, then those who preach against hunting must have been somehow abused or neglected in their upbringing as to cause them to intentionally deny their nature; or they are mutants missing the innate, genetic hunting desire altogether. In man's early days, they wouldn't have survived.

This might sound harsh, but it seems the only logical conclusion. I mean with all that's obviously "immoral" going on in the world today, how else can you explain the fixation of these fanatics on hunting?

The best solution I can give when you are asked by anti-hunting zealots to "prove hunting is right" or to "prove hunting is moral" is to turn the tables and demand that they prove to you hunting is wrong or immoral. It's a battle we never have to worry about losing, because they can't prove either.

Again, the bigger answer is, "We are the hunters—all of us," whether all of us admit it or not.

Who Are The Extreme Hunters?

Now, when you talk about "extreme hunting," that's another story. Extreme hunting is taking the innate hunting instinct to the tenth power. Extreme hunting is searching it, exploring it, wringing every drop of pleasure from that part of our nature. The reason the spectrum of emotions the hunter experiences is so broad is precisely because it is such a basal, deeply-rooted instinct.

A popular television commercial for Skeeter boats uses the simple slogan "Eat. Sleep. Fish." For the extreme hunter, "Eat. Sleep. HUNT!" pretty much sums life up in a nutshell, except that during the season all but minimal sleep is forsaken to traveling and scouting and hunting. Most meals in season are soggy sandwiches or gas station junk food shared evenly with the dog. The desire to hunt vastly overpowers the need for rest and sustenance.

The primary qualifica-tion for an extreme hunter

is that he or she is a hunter 365 days a year, not just during the season. Extreme hunting is a year-round lifestyle and is motivation for decisions in every other aspect of life. Where you live, how you invest your money, who you choose as a spouse, what you do for a living are all decisions partially based on how they will affect your hunting.

Waterfowl Hunting Has It All

To be certain, most any type of hunting can be experienced at the "extreme" level. The participant just has to commit himself or herself to a level of near fanaticism. Remember, "fan" as applied to any sport is short for fanatic.

Yet it seems easier to take waterfowl hunting to the realm of the extreme because, more than any other hunting sport, waterfowling is mystifyingly complex. To put it succinctly, waterfowl hunting has it all!

For example, hunting puddle ducks requires specialized wing-shooting skills, which, when performed well, are true athleticism with grace and fluidity matching the feats of any figure skater. The selection and placement of decoys involves strategies and variables that would confound Deep Blue, the chess playing computer from IBM. Beyond that there is calling, dog training

The smile and obvious pride in his canine hunting companion give it away! This guy is an extreme waterfowl hunter. This particular extreme waterfowler is largely responsible for this book being written—he's the author's father.

and handling, shotshell and firearm technology, seamanship and a dozen other intricacies, any one of which taken alone could easily require a lifetime to truly master.

Simply change the game to diving ducks or sea ducks or geese or sandhill cranes or swans, and it's easy to see how the pursuit of perfection in each can become an obsession. Though perfection in hunting is forever out of reach, it's the pursuit of it that keeps the extreme hunter coming back morning after morning.

The Creed Of Extreme Waterfowl Hunting

The extreme waterfowl hunter lives by a different set of rules than his average hunting siblings. The extreme waterfowler puts his or her all into every minute of every hunt. To the extreme waterfowler, duck and goose hunting is far more than a pastime: it's quite simply an everyday lifestyle. It's not lived only during a puny 50-, 60-, 70- or even 90-day waterfowl season. Extreme waterfowling is lived 365 days per year. One o'clock in the morning on the third of June is as likely to find an extreme waterfowler thinking about better ways to decoy ducks as are the final seconds before legal shooting on opening morning!

For the extreme waterfowl hunter, no chance of fooling a duck or a goose is too remote to preclude maximum effort. Though hunting is not hunting without the chance to kill game, taking a limit or even killing a single bird is not "the reason" for extreme hunting. It is, instead, to feel the rush of being close, within killing distance of a creature as magnificent as a duck or goose. It is to develop an instinctive understanding of your prey's habits and habitat that allows you to use its own preferences to bring it, against its will, so close that you can feel the air rushing between its feathers. It is having the game that close and having the final say as to whether it lives or dies. It is working with the conditions that Mother Nature dictates and knowing that if you make a bad decision, the cost might be the ultimate price. The rush comes from mastery of destiny—your own and the game's.

Extreme waterfowl hunting is not as much about collecting limits as it is about collecting experiences. To have taken ducks with a treasured old shotgun or with decoys of your own design, or tough retrieves made by a dog you trained yourself are far more important than to take a limit of birds in the same old way you've done it 100 or 1,000 times before.

While there's little doubt that the market hunters of 100 years ago met some of the criteria as extreme hunters, their motives did not. Today, waterfowl hunting to put meat on the table is not economically efficient. Even if it were, waterfowl hunters—the world's greatest and most magnanimous conservationists—have demanded wise possession limits which preclude stock-piling a year's supply of wild ducks in the freezer or salt barrel.

Ducks, geese, any game animals for that matter, deserve more than a future as nutrition for a hunter or his family. Yes, that's part of the reason we hunt, but, especially for the extreme hunter, there has to be more. No game animal, from a tiny woodcock to the biggest moose, should be taken unless it is going to create fine memories as well as fine dining.

The extreme hunter honors that code by taking only that game which comes on his or her terms. For the upland bird hunter that might mean only taking birds that are flushed by the hunter from in front of a solid point, not those stumbled across along the way. For the deer hunter it might mean taking only those deer spotted and stalked or only shooting a particular mature buck.

For the extreme waterfowl hunter it might mean taking only birds with their feet out, wings pumping backward, ready to land in the decoys. Maybe it's not going hunting when the dog is under the weather. Whatever the self-imposed challenges set inside what the law allows, it definitely means only shooting birds that will live long in the hunter's memory.

Rules To Live By

These are a few examples of views on waterfowl hunting that can indicate whether you fit the classification of extreme waterfowl hunter.

No price is too great to be hunting. Before the resurgence of duck populations in the 1990s, North American waterfowl hunters faced three-bird limits in some places, and some species were restricted to one or none. It was the extreme waterfowl hunters who kept the game alive. They maintained hunting camps, fed and trained retrievers year-round, bought enough ammo to keep the big companies still interested in research and development of better non-toxic loads.

Extreme waterfowl hunters don't complain about increased license or stamp prices. They don't mind outfitters trying to make a

Some wood ducks and teal contributed to a successful outing, but the smiles are even more because of the great memories this day turned out. Collecting experiences is what extreme hunting is all about.

decent living off of the services they provide. It's just part of the monetary price you have to pay to experience waterfowl hunting.

Extreme waterfowl hunters know that the greatest threat to ducks and geese and cranes and swans is loss of habitat. The threats to habitat are economic. The only way to see to it that critical habitat is not destroyed is for waterfowl to somehow pay its way. Since there aren't any paychecks in the avian world, the difference has to be made up by hunters, or it won't get done. The true extreme waterfowler buys an extra duck stamp or two every year and donates generously in time and money to waterfowl conservation organizations like

Ducks Unlimited, Waterfowl USA, the Delta Foundation and Wildlife Forever.

No effort is too great to be hunting. These days, die-hard snow goose hunters are the perfect example. They wake up earlier to put out and take in bigger decoy spreads of high-tech, high-priced decoys than ever before. They travel farther in pursuit of unhunted fields. They call louder and longer than ever before. They pit in or build more complex blinds than ever before.

They do all this to hunt birds, which, despite becoming more abundant each season, are exponentially more wary each season. The snow goose hunter's chances of taking a limit or even a few birds are lower than ever before despite improved technology and increasing effort! Yet they are out there, every day, all day, pitting reason against instinct. It's the challenge and the fickleness of the birds that actually inspire the extreme snow goose hunter.

Extreme waterfowlers will do whatever it takes to get to the birds. This is a tundra buggy used to transport hunters out to distant tidal flat blinds on the shores of Hudson Bay north of Churchill, Manitoba.

All extreme waterfowling is maximum effort waterfowling ... all day, every day. It's almost as if the extreme waterfowl hunter holds the belief that there can be no pleasure without pain.

No detail is too small to be ignored. The best place to see this is in an extreme waterfowler's decoy rig. First off, the rig changes from year to year as new and better decoys are developed. He or she may have a bent for nostalgia and keep a few special hand-carved or homemade dekes in the spread, but the vast majority will be high-tech, super-detailed fakes with state-of-the-art attractant technology. Unchippable paint and prototype finishes are de rigueur. The search to improve the pull, to bring birds closer, to take a bird by grabbing it out of the air is unrelenting.

The extreme waterfowler is always a fanatic about hiding from birds. No gun, no blind, no clothing, no single piece of gear can be suspect of sending a glint skyward to warn incoming birds. Likely his or her favorite color is marsh brown or corn stalk brown or olive drab or gun ship gray—all in flat, no-sheen finishes. Though the eyes of the extreme waterfowl hunter shine at the thought that you might want to hear about his or her last hunt, all that glistens is within— never on the exterior of hunter, dog or gear!

No location is too exotic. Because the motive for extreme waterfowl hunting is primarily the collection of experiences, the devotee knows that one must go where he or she must to gather them. We all dream of "skies darkened by flocks of decoying birds." To see them, to experience them, extreme waterfowlers will travel to roadless destinations like Churchill, Manitoba. We'll scrimp and save to see if the legends of Uruguay and Argentina are true. We'll sit still for hours straight in the tight confines of the equivalent of a refrigerator to experience sinkbox hunting in Quebec's St. Lawrence River. Rumors of great duck and goose hunting in places like Egypt and Siberia launch dreams that keep us awake at night scheming for ways to make them become reality.

No weather is too foul. The time we get to hunt ducks and geese is too limited as it is. You can't give up days just because the weather is less than optimal. That means sticking it out on the bluest of bluebird days and pushing it to the edge on the foulest of nasty days. Ice can be broken, even chopped if necessary. Snow storms can be driven through if you leave home early enough. A bigger, deeper boat and more powerful outboard can handle bigger waves.

Not mud, nor rain, nor cold shall keep the extreme waterfowl hunter from his enjoyment of the day and and the addition of new experiences to his life's collection!

Yes, common sense comes into play. The extreme waterfowler doesn't take fool chances because more than anything else he or she wants to survive to hunt again another day. But that doesn't mean that 90 percent or more of the time you can't work around the weather. If it's blowing too hard to put out your diver spread on the big water, then somewhere nearby geese will likely be looking for an easy field to feed in!

Extreme waterfowlers know they can't beat Mother Nature head on, but they always have several tricks up the sleeve to work around her!

The Collection Of Experiences

Many an extreme waterfowl hunter longs for a collection of mounted birds taken on his or her hunts. A pair of each species from each continent might be the mother of all extreme waterfowling goals. For a few it might be actually attainable, but for most of us it's just a dream. We'll be happy with perhaps a few special mounts, a stack of photographs, some well-thumbed hunting journals and ... most of all ... the memories. For a true extreme hunter, it's not the physical collection of the duck carcasses that is the driving force, it's the collection of the experiences they represent.

No other type of hunting can be done in the variety of places, under the diversity of conditions, at more polarized economic and societal levels than duck hunting. The extreme waterfowl hunter's true goal is to try it all.

Think of how many ways and places there are to take mallards alone! You can hunt them over decoys or by jump shooting them on the tidal pools and tundra ponds of Hudson Bay. In the prairie provinces you can hunt them on marshes, on bays off of big water or pouring into wheat or barley fields. You can pass shoot or decoy shoot or jump shoot. You can take mallards at multi-million-dollar duck clubs in California or by wading farther than the next guy on public marshes on the shores of Lake Erie. East Coast salt marshes have mallards, too. Arkansas is famous for both rice field and flooded timber mallard hunting. Texas has mallards; so does Florida; and Mexico, too. And we skipped slough hunting in North Dakota and field hunting in North Dakota and marsh hunting in Wisconsin and field hunting in Iowa. ... The fact is, mallards can be taken in at least 49 of the 50 states (Hawaii is not the paradise it's made out to be, at least for the extreme waterfowl hunter.)

The extreme waterfowl hunter wants to experience all of it. Every minute of it. Every sight, sound and sensation of every way and place there is to hunt ducks and geese. Extreme waterfowl hunting doesn't have to be hard, but it often is. It doesn't have to be expensive, but sometimes it is. It doesn't have to be spartan, but sometimes it is. At one time or another waterfowl hunting has to be all of these and more or less if it is to be experienced in its full spectrum.

Extreme waterfowl hunting is about collecting experiences and always having more to collect.

Extreme Waterfowl Hunting Is A Lifestyle

Taken to the extreme level, waterfowl hunting is more than a hobby. It's more than a pastime. It's even more than an avocation. Waterfowl hunting is a year-round, day-in-day-out lifestyle. It has to be. Retrievers don't disappear after the final hour of the season, only to reappear moments before opener. Wingshooting skills aren't earned and maintained in short courses during the season. Boats and decoys don't rig and paint themselves.

Besides the accumulation and obsessive maintenance of hunting gear, it's easy to spot the extreme waterfowler by the items with which he or she chooses to surround himself or herself in day to day life. Yes, paintings and prints and home decorations featuring subjects other than ducks and geese do exist. Yes, a mailbox will serve the same purpose if it doesn't sport a Canada goose landing or a mallard taking flight. Won't a fireplace poker roll logs and bank the fire just as well without a duck's head handle? Might there be other reasons besides bringing in ducks and geese that the Labrador retriever is America's most popular breed of dog? And the laws of gravity and physics will probably keep a stone fireplace hearth in place without the added weight of favorite old gunning decoys on top.

Yet, the extreme waterfowl hunter is oblivious to all of this. To him, if a toothbrush can't be had in mallard drake's head green, it's not a necessary tool except that it could probably be used to scrub the action on a semi-auto shotgun to keep it functioning smoothly in a flooded rice field.

To The Waterfowl Hunter Who Isn't Extreme ... Yet

Truth be told, there are practically no waterfowl hunters who meet all the qualifications of "extreme" all of the time. We'd like to think we do. We'd actually like to be, but the outside demands of "the modern world" make living the extreme life almost impossible.

Most of us drift in and out of the extreme classification. We meet some of the criteria all of the time and all of the criteria some of the time.

So don't be put off if you don't consider yourself an extreme waterfowl hunter. At times you probably are! And there are times when none of us want to be.

But every waterfowl hunter can learn from the tactics and experiences of the extreme hunters. They are like the formula race cars of the hunting world. They try stuff. They test stuff. They have the knowledge of a lifetime spent in the mud that can create innovations. What they create and discover will allow all of us to enjoy greater success in the pursuit of ducks and geese and in the pursuit of waterfowl hunting experiences. And after all, that is what it's all about for extreme hunter and non-extreme hunter alike.

Women can be just as extreme about waterfowl hunting as men. Sometimes they have better attention to detail and more patience than their male counterparts!

2

Guns of the
Extreme Waterfowler

*I*f the weather and field conditions are huntable—by any imaginable method or conveyance—the extreme waterfowl hunter *will be* hunting. It's the nature of the beast. He or she will not be held back by equipment that won't reliably function under the most difficult and adverse conditions. The extreme waterfowler's shotgun might fail once (which is okay because in the true extreme waterfowl hunter's boat or blind there will always be a back-up close at hand), but it will never fail twice ... because it won't be given the chance!

It might be said that the attitude of the extreme waterfowl hunter toward shotguns is "It works, or it goes." Hunting time is too precious to waste on babying a finicky firearm!

As you might guess, the extreme waterfowl hunter is likely the type of person who tries to determine the facts for himself or herself before selecting any piece of gear, especially one so integral to the hunt's success as a shotgun. Then those conclusions are put to the test where the pellets meet the plumage!

To help you with the selection of your next "best" waterfowling shooting iron, let's make a cold, deliberate comparison of the attributes that make up an extreme waterfowl hunting shotgun.

What Gauge?

With the requirement for non-toxic shot now universal for North American waterfowl hunters, there really are only two gauges to consider as every day hunting tools: the 12 gauge and the 10 gauge. Within the 12 gauge classification you need to consider a standard 3-inch magnum gun versus the relatively new 3½-inch magnum. The 10, of course, is standard in 3½-inch magnum, and that length is the only one in which you'll find 10 gauge shells commercially available.

Back when the 12 gauge 3½-inch guns started hitting the market, I got to pondering which of the "roman candles" would be the better extreme waterfowling shotshell and gun combination. I wanted to put the 12 gauge 3½-inch magnum and the 10 gauge 3½-inch magnum to a side-by-side field test. Though the results would be anecdotal rather than purely scientific, I figured that would be okay since the extreme waterfowler usually makes final decisions based on first-hand experience anyway.

A fair head-to-head test required guns as similar as possible to one another, the only difference being the chambering. That meant the Browning BPS pump was the perfect subject since it's available in both gauges. Paul Thompson at Browning helped by consigning me two BPS pumps to shoot head-to-head.

The guns Paul provided were identical in every detail. Both were the BPS Stalker version with dull metal finish and black, synthetic stocks. Both had 30-inch barrels equipped with the Invector choke tube system. Both featured the goose-blind-smart bottom ejection for which the BPS is known.

The only difference between the two was that one was chambered for 10 gauge magnum; the other for 12 gauge 3½-inch magnum.

At the patterning board, both guns did themselves proud with the choke tubes provided. As could be expected, the best large shot size (BBB and T) steel patterns were achieved through lead modified tubes.

In comparing published ballistics, the 10 gauge and the 12 gauge 3½-inch stack up pretty evenly. In steel shells, the difference in the heaviest loads of big shot is just ¹⁄₁₆ ounce in favor of the 10. That's only a few pellets in sizes like BBB, T and F.

Theoretically, the 10 gauge has an advantage. It is commonly believed that a shot string that starts short in the shell stays short. Obviously, to fit the same amount of shot in a 12 gauge shell of smaller diameter rather than the wider 10 gauge shell the payload must create a longer cylinder in the hull.

While flooded timber hunting conditions don't usually call for a 10 gauge gun, if you use steel shot and shoot the gun well, a Remington SP-10 makes a fine all-around waterfowling gun.

On the other end of the gauge spectrum, this is the reason 28 gauge lovers tout their guns over the .410. Though the two can be loaded similarly, the shortened shot string produced by the 28 gives much greater satisfaction on the skeet range by "smoking" targets the .410 might only break.

Hunters with 10s and 12s find success side by side as shown on this early season goose hunt.

The best testing opportunity for the two Brownings was a season of goose and duck hunting with them. On many mornings that fall, several hunting companions and I took the guns out to the same blind on the same morning. Between shooting opportunities we would switch guns, so that each shooter had the chance to make "next shot" comparisons in actual hunting situations.

On a number of occasions, I also loaned one or the other of the guns to a number of other hunters to get their opinions.

At best, the results were consistent, but inconclusive. Everyone made positive comments about the guns, but none made any remarks about the difference in the performance of the gauges—with one exception. Both of them killed ducks and geese pretty dead!

Every person who shot both guns (including myself) and those who only had the opportunity to shoot the 12 gauge 3½-inch noted how hard the 12 kicked with the heavy loads. The difference, as with any gun of any gauge or caliber, was most notable when pattern testing from a bench.

The 10 certainly has plenty of juice, but the 12 gauge 3½-inch's recoil "feels" even more jarring. Since the guns were nearly identical in weight, it has to have something to do with the physics of the gauge/load configuration.

Since the season of informal testing, I've also talked to a lot of other gun writers about their experiences with the 12 gauge 3½-inch magnum. Totally unsolicited words like "kick," "recoil," "punch," and some unprintable ones arose in every conversation.

On an aside, there is nothing "macho" about being able to handle recoil! Heavy recoil is a dual defeating proposition. If you're uncomfortable shooting a gun, you won't shoot it nearly as often as you should. If you "aren't bothered" by heavy recoil and you do shoot a lot with hard kicking guns, you may pay the price down the road. Eye problems such as detached retinas, as well as chronic bone and joint pains, can be directly traceable to a lifetime of shooting heavy recoiling firearms. There's also a growing belief that heavy recoil to the skeletal system may play a role in causing long-term hearing loss.

Shoot the lowest recoiling load that is appropriate to the hunting you'll be doing. In tight confines, even your hunting partner will appreciate it.

Much of the marketing hype of the 12 gauge 3½-inch chambered shotgun is a fallacy. They are not the perfect "all-around" shotgun! Look carefully.

A shotgun with enough weight to reduce the felt recoil of the 3½-inch 12 gauge or 10 gauge is really useful only in a stationary hunting situation, i.e. a goose pit. Just for kicks, I tried hunting grouse and jump shooting ducks with the Browning BPS 12, 3½ loaded with 2¾-inch shells. It was an experience in pumping iron that I do want to repeat! Likewise I've carried an Remington SP 10 on turkey hunts and found it uncomfortable in short order.

On the other hand, the 3½-inch 12 is certainly chambered in some lighter guns, but I value my retinas more than to shoot a single, maximum load shell once a year. That makes taking even one limit of geese rather difficult.

The 3½-inch magnums, in both 10 gauge and 12 gauge are guns/loads that were created for the waterfowler. The 10 gauge was popular in olden days because with blackpowder, more was definitely better. As smokeless powder and shotshell technology advanced, the mighty 10 faded from the picture. For many years, commercially available guns and loads were few and far between. The 10 gauge had a resurgence of popularity when steel shot became the law of the land, making bigger definitely better again.

The 12 gauge 3½-inch on the other hand, is a relatively new creation. Its supposed niche is to give the all-around hunter one 12 gauge shotgun with which he can do all of his hunting most effectively regardless of the load—from the heaviest steel magnums to the lightest dove loads. However, the weight and resultant recoil issues—especially when you're talking about 3½-inch magnum lead turkey loads—leave most believing that a 12 gauge 3½-inch is a specialty gun for extreme waterfowlers.

Yet there is another that most certainly contends for the title of the greatest extreme waterfowling firearm. Don't pass over the standard 12 gauge 3-inch magnum! Shotguns so chambered have taken millions and millions of waterfowl and will do so for many decades to come. The only reason that the 3½-inch magnums have taken center stage is because early non-toxic loads were somewhat lacking. The way to achieve improved performance with steel loads of years past was to move up to a "roman candle."

That's not the case anymore! Tungsten combinations, bismuth shot and state-of-the-art, super high velocity steel loads make the

2¾- and 3-inch 12 gauge an acceptable, actually preferable, choice for extreme waterfowl hunting. In some hunting situations, it's possible to make a case that the 12 gauge tungsten loads offer better performance than lead ever did, but that's getting ahead of the story. The next chapter will reveal the history and future of non-toxic shotshells for the extreme waterfowl hunter.

In the choice of gauge for your next extreme waterfowling shotgun, consider this: If you plan on sticking with steel at least until a economically priced non-toxic alternative is developed, and if you frequently hunt large, tough, maximum range birds like snow geese, giant Canadas, cranes and tundra swans, then compare your options in 10 gauge and 12 gauge 3½-inch magnum guns, buy one and don't look back.

If however, you are willing and financially able to select your shells carefully and commit to shooting only the top of the line, high-speed steel primarily at ducks, and if you are willing to shell out the extra coin to buy the tungsten or bismuth loads when the situation demands it, then it's a darn good bet you'll live happily ever after with a standard 12 gauge 3-inch magnum—and you'll be shooting lighter recoiling 2¾-inch shells much of the time to boot!

What About Ultralight Hunting?

Too often the comparison is made between ultralight fishing and various forms of hunting. Yes, it is more sporting to take fish on whippy rods and light line. And at first thought it might, indeed, seem like more extreme hunting to use a 20 gauge in the goose pit. But there's a big difference.

A fish taken on ultralight gear is more than likely to be released after some careful resuscitation when the fight is over. If it's lost during the course of the battle, there's every reason to believe that it will recover quickly to live a perfectly normal, pain free life.

On the other hand, when you make the decision to pull up and shoot the goose, your intent is to kill it dead, where it flies, with one shot. In one instant it's alive, in the next it's dead with nothing in between—no pain, no recognition. Because we are launching a sequence of events that's irreversible, we owe our game maximum effort to make the kill as instantaneous and humane as possible.

In other words, there is no such thing as over kill. Dead is dead. Game can't be too dead. It can't be killed too quickly once the shot is taken.

Selection of an extreme waterfowling shotgun must be based largely on its reliability—even in the toughest conditions—and how much effort you're willing to put into the care of the gun.

The extreme waterfowler's selection of gauge is based on logic and reasoning. Use the gun that you believe gives you the best opportunity to make a clean kill under the most difficult conditions. It's just as foolish to go to the blind under-gunned as it is to go over-gunned. There's nothing macho about shooting geese with too small a gun, because eventually something beyond your control will go awry, and you'll needlessly leave a bird to suffer and feed the coyotes. More is the pity because you could have prevented it by selecting a more appropriate gun and load.

As a committed extreme waterfowl hunter, your combination of experience and conscience will tell you what's right.

What Action?

The selection of action-type for the extreme waterfowling shotgun is almost as complex as the choice of gauge is simple. Extreme waterfowlers use single-shots, bolt-actions, double barrels, pumps and semi-autos of innumerable makes and models to take ducks, geese, coot, swans and cranes every season. And likely they'll continue to do so for many seasons to come. However, if your search is for the "best" or the "ultimate" extreme waterfowling gun, then you have to start the separation of chaff from grain somewhere. Again, the way to do it is analyze the facts, make a decision, then test it in the field. It's the way the extreme waterfowl hunter selects his gear.

The factors to consider are reliability, ease of care, handling qualities inherent to the action and, that most subjective of all, personal appeal or esthetics. Each type of action offers specific advantages or disadvantages in each of these areas.

Single-Shots. There's a lot to be said for starting a beginning hunter, no matter his or her age, with a single-shot shotgun no matter what type of hunting the novice will be doing. The greatest advantage is safety. If the neophyte has the makings of an extreme waterfowl hunter, he or she is going to be excited in the blind and even more excited when that first duck falls. The excitement can be so overpowering, the beginner might momentarily forget about the responsibilities of handling a loaded gun. With only one shot to begin with, the gun's no longer loaded when the duck's kicking its last.

Light weight might be considered another of the single-shot's merits, but when shooting heavy loads, especially for a hunter of slighter build, the recoil of a light, break-action gun becomes a noticeable and sometimes intolerable liability. The substantial felt recoil can hurt the development of solid shooting skills and it can just plain hurt! Balance in the type of single-shots you're likely to find in duck blinds and goose pits probably won't be the greatest either—another deterrent to the development of solid wingshooting basics.

The low initial cost of a single-shot shotgun is another advantage for starting the beginner. You can buy one relatively inexpensively, so you're not out a great deal if the beginner determines he or she likes bungee jumping or street luging better than waterfowl hunting. However, most of the economically priced singles intended for hunting use are hammer-type guns that can be difficult for very young hands to cock when game is in view.

I can remember some of my own earliest bird hunts on which I was allowed to carry a shotgun. While that Savage/Stevens 28 gauge had worked great on squirrels, my earliest upland bird and duck hunts (back in the days of lead shot) left me near tears because my small thumbs weren't strong enough to cock the hammer in time to catch a speeding target.

The Texas goose fields are one of the toughest tests for a waterfowling shotgun. This group did all right with a combination of pumps and autos. No, they're not camera shy; there are more birds comin' in!

While a single-shot requires minimal investment to find out whether you have a budding extreme waterfowl hunter or not, they generally can't be considered a lifetime gun. A beginning hunter will almost certainly want to step up to some kind of repeater as his or her hunting and wingshooting skills blossom. So a semi-auto or a pump with ammunition conscientiously doled out one shot at a time will provide the same safety net during the early hunts and still meet the desires as experience grows.

Ultimately, single-shots must be rated high on the reliability scale. There are few moving parts and if something does go wrong, a good share of the action is right there for you to look at and possibly repair in the field. Working on some types of semi-autos or, God forbid, a double-barreled gun in the goose pit, can be akin to disassembling a Swiss watch while participating in a mud wrestling match!

Double Barrels. The waterfowling guns of North America's legendary extreme waterfowlers were double barrels. Perhaps most famous among them were Bo Whoop I and Bo Whoop II, the side-by-sides that made history in the hands of Nash Buckingham. Today's waterfowling doubles are primarily over/unders, though the development of bismuth shot and the tungsten-polymer blends have made it possible to again hunt ducks and geese with those great old side-by-sides.

The greatest advantage the double barrel offers to the extreme waterfowl hunter is reliability. Very little can go wrong that will prevent a double gun from firing. The problem is when something does go wrong, it's usually some kind of catastrophic failure that will require a competent gunsmith with a complete shop, specialized tools and maybe some hard-to-get parts to repair. Yet if only one barrel is out of commission, you're still in the hunt. Because their action and lock mechanisms are so "enclosed," it's difficult for dirt or moisture to enter the guts of a double. Yet when it does, it's equally difficult to get it out.

Like single-shots, double guns tend to kick harder than pump or semi-auto guns because there are no moving parts to absorb the recoil or spread it out over a longer time curve. Recoil from heavy loads in a double gun at least "feels" more severe because it's administered in a short, sharp blow rather than an elongated push. However, it is less than a single-shot because there's more mass in the double's second barrel and usually receiver and stock to boot, which absorbs some of the recoil and reduces muzzle jump.

Double barrels of both persuasions are renowned for fine balance, though in reality the definition of shotgun balance is how it feels to the shooter. To many American shooters, pumps or semi-autos "feel" better than doubles. However, the best shotgunners in the world in games that require second shots, almost exclusively use over/under guns. The reason is the combination of reliability and balance.

In high-quality doubles of the type desirable to an extreme water-fowl hunter, cost is one big disadvantage. They are far and away the most expensive option and quite often you're paying for fluff like engraving and fancy wood. It's hard, even for the most extreme of extreme waterfowlers, to take cans of black and olive drab spray paint to a beautiful shotgun for which he just paid the equivalent of a season's lease on a California rice field blind!

One big advantage of shooting a double barrel for mixed bag waterfowl hunting is the fact that you can have instant selection between two loads and two chokes. Your open barrel could be loaded with, say bismuth #5s for the mallards decoying like they are supposed to. The tighter barrel could be stuffed with a high velocity BBB 3-inch shell in preparation for a Canada goose that might fly by. Only those hunters extreme enough to become adept with double-trigger guns usually make use of this advantage in field hunting situations where birds flush unexpectedly and the decision on which barrel to use has to be made instinctively. However, in the blind setting where there's usually a lapse of time between spotting the birds and shooting, it's easy to make a conscious decision even with a single, selective trigger.

Yet it's in the confines of a blind, particularly a small pit blind, where another disadvantage to a double gun, particularly stack-barreled guns, rears its head. Breaking open an over/under is an easy, natural act in the field. In a tight blind, it can be a time-consuming exercise in contortions. The gun has to be broken so far to eject and insert shells that oftentimes the barrels must be pointed skyward over the walls of a blind to do it. Defying the laws of gravity while closing the inverted action is a skill that must be developed by the extreme waterfowl hunter who hunts with a double gun.

Pumps. The pump action shotgun is the stalwart of America's extreme waterfowl hunters. Legendary pumps like the Winchester Model 12 and the Remington 870 have seen to that. They are rugged and reliable. A good pump with a synthetic stock could likely be pressed into service as a canoe paddle on the way to the blind and still shoot when it got there!

Though they don't offer the instant load choice of the double, it's still pretty quick to pop open a pump and load a couple of BBBs into the chamber and magazine when the Canadas start eyeing your mallard spread.

Interchangeable choke tubes have made just about any action a justifiable choice as "the all-around" shotgun, but modern pumps allow you to change the barrel completely, if you wish, for

Shooting from boats and floating blinds adds a whole new dimension to wingshooting and shotgun selection.

different types of shooting and hunting. The extreme waterfowler is likely to have a couple of barrels just for different waterfowl hunting situations.

Of the repeaters, pump action guns are the least expensive but are available in a pretty wide price range depending on what you want in a gun. At the bottom end, some extreme waterfowl guides who spend anywhere from 90 to 150 days a year helping their hunters find ducks and geese look on inexpensive pumps as disposable guns. They'll buy a Remington 870 Express, for example, with the idea that it will last one season, maybe two. From the day it's taken to the range to check some patterns, the gun is never cleaned, never oiled. If it should be dropped muzzle in the mud, it's quickly disassembled, the clog blown or pushed from the barrel, then reassembled to hunt again. For the professional extreme waterfowl hunter those hours saved of not having to clean a gun every night are worth the $200 to $250 a year a new gun costs.

A quality-built, well-maintained pump gun can stand up to a lifetime of extreme waterfowl hunting.

On the other hand, a well-maintained pump can last a lifetime or several lifetimes. One of my own prized extreme waterfowling guns is a Remington 870 that was made in the early 1950s; right at the time Remington started chambering the vent rib models in 3-inch. It was my dad's only shotgun for 30 years, and I've put tens of thousands of rounds through it hunting and target shooting. Though it's semi-retired today because I have other guns I shoot better and because it is choked awfully tight for most modern waterfowl loads, it has become tradition that I take Dad's gun out each opening day and shoot the first ducks of the year with it. Yet it could still provide many more seasons as my one and only extreme waterfowling gun because the care it received after each day of hunting was and is meticulous.

Pumps are easy and quick to load and unload even in a blind that fits like a body suit. Some, like the Browning BPS, offer the added benefit of bottom ejection. This prevents flying empties from crossing your partner's line of sight or landing in his or her hood. It also leaves empty hulls in a small, easily picked-up pile at your feet. That's an advantage because it saves you wading to pick up floating hulls that can spook wary birds. And finally, bottom ejection makes one gun truly ambidextrous for any shooter—no shells whizzing past the nose of the lefty using a right-handed gun.

Though it varies with make and model, pumps are usually pretty simple to strip down, even in the field, if they turn up with an unlikely problem. More than one pump's trigger group has been pulled out right in the blind, blown on to remove crud or melt some ice, then popped back into place to perform without further problems. The tool is usually a Leatherman tool or something even less likely to be seen on a fine gunsmith's bench!

Recoil, even from the heaviest loads, is more tolerable in a pump than in the break-action guns of similar weight because the shooter utilizes part of the recoil to begin the motion of cycling the pump. Balance is usually somewhat weight-forward in an extreme waterfowling pump gun, so this also helps reduce felt recoil and muzzle jump.

Extreme waterfowl hunters who shoot pump guns can shoot and cycle their guns about as fast as the shooter of a semi-auto, but speed seldom means much. You can shoot as fast as you want, but if the gun's not pointed in exactly the right place, you won't hit a thing! Overall, it's a bit easier to learn to make second and third shots count with a semi-auto simply because there is nothing to distract the shooter from concentrating on the target. However, many extreme waterfowlers believe that the longer learning curve in shooting a pump is well worth the added reliability a pump gun provides!

Semi-automatics. "Autos" or "automatics," as they are frequently called, should be the number-one choice of extreme waterfowl hunters, except for one thing. They have a bad, but largely un-deserved, reputation for being unreliable.

Let's look at all the pluses first. Semi-autos use gas or recoil itself to cycle the action. That cuts down on felt recoil from even the heaviest loads more than any other action type. They tend to balance better or feel better to most shooters. Semi-autos are easy to shoot and easy to learn to shoot. They are available from more mainstream manufacturers than any other action. Price is middle of the road—higher than pumps, lower than most doubles. They can most easily be classified as the all-around shotgun for those who consider that quality an attribute.

Okay, that leaves reliability. Modern semi-automatic shotguns are extremely reliable, with one caveat. You have to do your part.

Your part is keeping them clean, maintaining them well, and shooting them properly. That sounds like a lot, especially to the "never clean 'em" pump shooter, but it's really not a big deal.

To hunt happily ever after with an auto, follow these three simple steps:

1) Thoroughly clean the gun after *each* day of hunting. That doesn't mean just to wipe down the outside with a silicone cloth. Take the gun apart to its main component groups. Use brushes and chemicals and elbow grease to remove whatever fouling you can find. If it has been a particularly muddy or dusty hunt, pull the trigger group and blow it clean with a compressor or canned air. Before reassembly, wipe all surfaces with a *lightly, lightly, lightly* oiled cloth. Too much oil is a major contributor to semi-auto malfunctions.

2) Before reassembly, carefully inspect all parts that can wear. Carry replacements of frangible parts like rubber o-rings, etc. Replace them generously, even if they *look* like they are *starting* to wear.

3) Know what loads pattern and function best in your gun. Shoot the gun with it solidly rested against your shoulder.

The extreme waterfowler who knows firsthand the kind of wing-shooting magic that can be performed with a quality semi-automatic shotgun is willing to live by the old gun fighter's code: *"You take care of your guns, and they'll take care of you!"*

And how!

There's Beauty In Balance

For the extreme waterfowl hunter, the search for the perfect shotgun or shotguns entails two basic criteria. First, he or she must have a gun that can be relied upon day-in and day-out, no matter how severe the conditions. If the cold and wet and snow and mud are humanly tolerable, then the shotgun must perform. Secondly, the extreme hunter is perpetually on the lookout for a shotgun he or she can shoot well ... and better than the one currently in use.

The ability to shoot a gun well relies on a great many variables of the gun and the hunter. When it's all condensed down, that means how a shotgun feels to the individual shooter. In a word, that's "balance."

The old axiom in the days of heavy lead loads using slow burning powder was that a waterfowl gun wasn't of much use unless it had a barrel of 30 or more inches. And while these are still fine shotguns, in many cases still in use today, they can never be what you'd call a well-balanced shotgun. New ideas are emerging in what sort of balance is best in the all-around hunting shotgun.

Factory camo finishes as on this Mossberg pump make a gun more useful to the extreme waterfowler and help it stand up to the elements with less care!

An Extreme Waterfowler Learns A Lesson

It was Halloween morning. True to the magic that can happen only on that day, the sky was blue, the sun was bright, yet there were snowflakes in the air. They sifted down like diamond dust, making the most of the sunlight until they melted into the surface of the lake.

The scene was beautiful. An artist couldn't have painted a prettier picture. The snow wasn't piling up on the backs of the dozen decoys out in front of me, so I welcomed the diversion of watching the drifting flakes between flocks of interested ducks and geese.

A goose and a greenhead already lay on the rocks beside me. Sadie's black coat still dripped from the swim out for the goose. It was a perfect morning; just the two of us. The guests of honor had yet to arrive.

As I reached into my gunning bag for the vacuum bottle of coffee, I heard the fanfare that announced their arrival. It was a roar to rival the space shuttle dropping through the earth's atmosphere, about to make its landing.

It was a flock of bluebills working this small lake like they usually do.

Commuting from bigger waters where they spend the night, the bluebills and ringbills and sometimes redheads and canvasbacks plummet straight down from heights where it's difficult to see them with the naked eye. They level off a dozen feet above the water and kick in the afterburners to make several laps of all the lake's irregular points and bays.

They spotted my string of fakes, adjusted formation and roared on in. I picked up my heirloom Remington 870 with its 30-inch barrel and steel magazine plug. It came to my shoulder like the part of my body it has become and urged me to pull the bead ahead of the drake in the lead. I did and slapped the trigger.

The formation of scaup pulled out, but the fifth and sixth ducks back cartwheeled then bounced across the water. Sadie gave an almost inaudible whine, and I sent her to pick them up.

While she went about her joyous business, I pulled another steel 3-inch #2 from my bag, pushed it into the bottom of the well-worn receiver and shook my head. Certainly I was happy about the two-for-one shot, which, had anybody been there to see it, I likely would have tried to convince them was on purpose.

What frustrated me was the fact that the barrel-heavy gun that I love so dearly lied to me. Its weight-out-front balance had prevented me from reaching the swing speed I needed to bust the intended 'bill 10 feet in front of the first one I hit!

Tradition has it that a waterfowling shotgun's weight is supposed to be out there in a right-handed shooter's left hand. The current trend is for longer barrels in sporting clays and even skeet shooting.

You can't argue with the laws of physics. A body set in motion tends to stay in motion. The heavier that body is, the greater the tendency.

That's what that weight out there toward the muzzle is supposed to do. It's supposed to help you keep the gun moving after you've hit the trigger, which is the absolute, number-one key to hitting what you're shooting at with a shotgun! Weight-forward guns do help you maintain your swing.

But in a situation like those bluebills roaring in on Halloween day, the shooter is called upon to pick his gun off the blind wall, mount it, swing it, establish enough lead to hit the bird he or she wants to hit, and keep the gun swinging fast enough to finish the task. That last bit, about swing speed, is where a front-heavy gun can hurt you.

Pass-shooting, where you see the birds coming for a long time, calculate lead and continue swinging, has long been the true-calling of shotguns with a weight-forward balance. Problem is, at least for me, I can't hit any kind of target if I think about it that much.

NAHC Life Member Leon Measures' "Shoot Where You Look" course taught me a much surer method of hitting those maximum range, look-at-'em-forever targets. Simply put, you don't shoulder the gun until you're ready to shoot. When the gun hits your shoulder, you're pulling the trigger. Coming up to swing-speed and establishing the proper lead is all accomplished while the gun's on its way to your shoulder. Once it gets there, all you have to do is touch the trigger and maintain the swing.

This style of wingshooting, whether it's done on 15-pound giant Canada geese at 45 yards or darting woodcock at 10 yards is the forte of a shotgun that is balanced with just a little extra weight in your front hand, or better yet, truly balanced with its center of gravity between your hands when the gun is mounted. This is, for lack of a better name, "the all-around shotgun."

Surprisingly, most any make or model of gun can come close to fitting this description. You simply adjust by selecting a barrel length that seems to put the balance of the gun in the middle, rather than forward of your front hand. If you try the same make and model with decreasing barrel lengths, you might be amazed at just how much difference a couple of inches makes.

One of my favorite waterfowling guns is a Remington SP-10 10 gauge autoloader. Admittedly, it's a heavy gun. I've taken it turkey hunting precisely once in the eight or nine years I've owned it. It's way too beefy to carry up and down all those hills. But when a boat or ATV can get it out to the blind for me, it's an awesome tool.

But despite its overall weight, I've found that the 26-inch barrel points and swings wonderfully for me. I tried a 30-inch barrel when I first bought the gun, and if I hadn't been able to switch to the shorter barrel, it might have ended up as a boat anchor!

Most of the guns featured here have interchangeable barrels available from the maker or from custom barrel makers, so you can experiment quite easily. In the case of double guns or old-timers, you should try to shoot a variety of barrel lengths before you buy—or be

Whichever shotgun action, brand and model you select, the most important consideration is learning to use it like an extension of your own body.

certain enough with what you want to accomplish to allow a gunsmith to whittle the barrels into balance inch by inch.

When Sadie reached my side with the second bluebill, I took the brace in my hand and admired them as I do most all game that I'm lucky enough to take. I marvel at waterfowl in particular because of their incredible annual travels. Just a day before, the ducks in my hand might have taken off somewhere on the prairies of Manitoba. My taking them on this special lake, with a special dog and a special gun and putting them on the dinner table for my family, to me defines the balance of nature. And who could argue the beauty in that!

Choke Selection

Telling an extreme waterfowler what choke constriction to use, these days, is akin to telling him or her who to choose as a wife or husband! The proper way to select the "best choke" is to court many of them until you find the ones that suit each of your hunting situations the best.

Before the days of easily changeable chokes, and before the mid-'90s quantum leap in non-toxic shot technology, the way to match a gun and load was to buy a variety of loads, test them at the pattern board and select the load that patterned the best. The selection process today is much different and, in a way, more reliable.

Today's extreme waterfowl hunter will study the attributes of various shot materials, velocities, payloads, brands, price and availability. Based on that research, it should be fairly easy to determine a load or group of similar loads that should provide the best results. Then, he or she will take the shotgun and a selection of interchangeable choke tubes to the range with a good supply of the selected load. Testing on patterning targets will prove which choke constriction provides the most consistent, even pattern at the distances at which shooting is anticipated.

That's how the determination should be made.

Choke Selection Hints

Because of the advances in powders, wads and hulls, as well as the wider variety of approved non-toxic shot materials, today's loads tend to pattern much tighter than those used by the extreme waterfowl hunters of lead and early steel shot days. That means modern loads will hit more frequently and kill more efficiently when fired through more open chokes than the old timers used.

For steel and tungsten-iron loads, begin your pattern testing with improved cylinder, skeet 2 or modified chokes. For bismuth or tungsten polymer loads, try starting with modified or improved modified constrictions. From your starting constriction, move out in either direction and compare results.

Be sure that the tubes you are using are recommended for all types of shot materials. Also, stick with the same brand and model of tubes for your head to head testing. Different firearms and tube manufacturers have different constriction specifications for tubes of the same name.

Meeting The Needs Of Extreme Waterfowlers

North American Hunter magazine Senior Editor Mike Faw recently polled all of North America's most popular shotgun makers for their recommendations on which shotguns best meet the needs of the extreme waterfowl hunter. In researching this story, Mike noted, "Extreme waterfowl hunting is sometimes a dirty job, but these guns love to do it!"

Here's what the mainstream makers recommend:

Beretta AL390 Synthetic. The black advanced polymer stock and forearm are reinforced with fiberglass on this durable hunting shotgun. A smooth, black matte finish from the rubber recoil pad to the muzzle cuts glare. It arrives sling ready with swivels. This gas operated 12 gauge autoloader shoots 2¾- and 3-inch shells.

Flush mounted internal screw-in Mobilchokes are steel shot proofed. The AL390 weighs 7½ pounds with four barrel length options. The barrels are made of nickel-chromium-molybdenum steel. An exclusive hard-chromed bore ensures truer, more consistent patterns and resists pitting and corrosion. Magazine cut-off allows easy unloading of the chamber or quick loading of a different load. Removable trigger group is easily cleaned, and the ambidextrous safety is reversible for left or right hand shooters. Contact: Beretta, Dept. NAH, 17601 Beretta Drive, Accokeek, MD 20607.

Browning Gold Hunter 3½ Field Model. Shotshell selection became much simpler with the introduction of Browning's Gold Hunter 3½-inch 12 gauge shotgun. This shotgun shoots all 2¾-, 3- and 3½-inch loads interchangeably.

"Extraordinary balance, uncanny pointability and smooth function" are the terms Browning uses to describe its Gold Hunter. This autoloader is a relatively light 7 pounds, 10 ounces. It's easy to take down quickly, even in the field. Even the trigger assembly can be removed and replaced in seconds. The opening in the trigger guard is larger to accommodate gloved fingers.

A back bored 28-inch 12 gauge barrel offers regulated gas operation. The shorter, lightweight advanced alloy receiver is finished with a durable, non-glare deep black coating. All other exposed metal parts are high-gloss finished.

An oversized triangular safety also provides reliable gloved-hand operation. A magazine cut-off feature lets you load ahead of the next shell in the magazine. Invector plus choke tubes and wrench included. A select walnut, full pistol grip stock and finger-grooved forearm provide a comfortable, solid feel in your hands. Contact: Browning, Dept. NAH, One Browning Place, Morgan, UT 84050.

New England Firearms SB2 (see photo next page). New England Firearms' (NEF) break-action 10 gauge shotgun combines quality and value. This shotgun has a 32-inch barrel chambered for up to 3½-inch magnum shells with a set, standard modified choke. A unique green and black camouflage pattern helps you blend in with the surroundings. The gold bead front sight finishes off the barrel tip and assists with target acquisition.

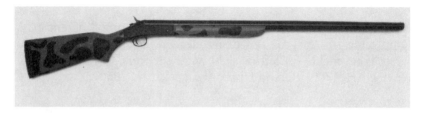

The NEF SB2 is built with an investment cast steel frame and will handle steel and other types of non-toxic shot interchangeably. Other features include a ventilated rubber recoil pad and automatic shell ejector. Comes complete with an adjustable nylon webbed sling, swivels and posts. NEF says that this shotgun is for the serious waterfowler who hunts in extreme conditions and wants the most carefree shotgun available with long-range performance. Contact: H&R 1871, Dept. NAH, Industrial Rowe, Gardner, MA 01440.

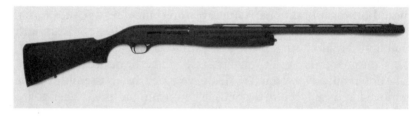

H&K Benelli M-1 Super 90. Benelli's famous Montefeltro inertia bolt system ensures dependable operation with all standard 12 gauge shells up to the most powerful 3-inch magnums. You can also remove or replace a shell in the chamber without emptying the magazine. This field shotgun sports a 26-inch barrel with a 3-inch chamber. The barrel is chrome lined with a corrosion-resistant finish.

The M-1 Super 90's high-strength black polymer stock and forearm are a dull matte finish and will not reveal your position to incoming waterfowl. The gun is also available in Realtree X-tra Brown camouflage and with a 28-inch barrel. The stepped vented ribbed barrel has a red front bead sight. Sling post provided on the forend cap. Contact: Heckler & Koch, Dept. NAH, 21480 Pacific Blvd., Sterling, VA 20166.

Mossberg Viking 835 Ulti-Mag. Viking shotguns can be quickly identified by their custom molded Viking green synthetic stocks and forends. This 12 gauge pump shotgun has a 28-inch factory ported barrel that offers a 3½-inch chamber and an extra-wide, full-length vent rib. Includes a brass bead at mid-barrel and a white bead front sight to ensure accurate target lineup.

Detachable swivel posts are installed front and rear so that a sling can be easily added. The unique and durable synthetic stock and forearm assist with concealment and can take the abuse of less-than-ideal hunting conditions. Other features include a Quiet-Carry forend, a gold trigger, rubber recoil pads and a 10-year warranty. Package includes cable lock to prevent operation of the action when you finish your hunt. Contact: O.F. Mossberg & Sons, Dept. NAH, 7 Grasso Ave., North Haven, CT 06473.

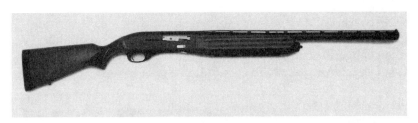

Remington SP-10 Magnum. The Remington SP-10 is a gas-operated 10 gauge with 3½-inch chambers that will deliver on ducks or geese. Available with 26- or 30-inch Rem-choke equipped, vented rib barrels with a white bead front sight. The American walnut stock has a satin finish and all exposed metal parts have a non-reflective matte finish to hide from wary waterfowl eyes. In fact, the model is also available in Mossy Oak Break-Up camouflage with a 23-inch barrel, supplied with full, modified and turkey extra-full chokes.

This shotgun's autoloading action helps reduce recoil to a level comparable with many 12 gauges. But the 10 gauge loads deliver up to 34 percent more pellets in the target area. A padded Cordura sling is included and attached to the post studs to help you comfortably take the firearm afield. Contact: Remington Arms, Dept. NAH, 870 Remington Drive, Madison, NC 27025.

Ruger Red Label. These over/under shotguns are engineered with American know-how! They feature back-bored 12 gauge barrels with 3-inch chambers providing softer felt recoil and uniform patterns. Barrel selection is incorporated in the sliding tang safety. Barrel length options exist, but waterfowlers will likely choose the 28-inch version. All Red Label barrels are hammer forged from chrome molybdenum steel with a gold sight bead affixed to the front. The barrels are stress relieved, contour ground, precisely fitted and silver soldered.

The standard Ruger Red Label has a smooth, 400-series stainless receiver, trigger and forend iron. The finely checkered stock and semi-beavertail forend are shaped from first-quality, straight-grained American walnut. Weight is approximately 7¾ pounds. Five interchangeable choke tubes are provided. Contact: Sturm, Ruger & Co., Dept. NAH, Lacey Place, Southport, CT 06490.

Weatherby Orion II Classic Field. This fine over/under waterfowling piece sports 12 gauge 30-inch barrels with full and modified choke tubes out ahead of the 3-inch chambers. Backboring reduces recoil and improves shot patterns. Its modified Greener crossbolt action is one of the strongest and most reliable.

Weatherby's Orion special breeching system provides seven points of engagement for a stronger, safer action. Automatic ejectors hurl spent shells upon opening and slightly raise unfired shells for easy removal. The vented rib is matte finished to reduce glare and help reduce barrel heat buildup. Patented sear block trigger prevents accidental discharge, and a sliding top safety prevents firing unless the top barrel release lever is fully closed.

Features a comfortable rounded pistol grip stock and attractive walnut wood on the beaver-tailed forend and stock. Finely engraved wildlife scenes on each side of the receiver. Includes extra choke and wrench. Contact: Weatherby, Dept. NAH, 3100 El Camino Real, Atascadero, CA 93422.

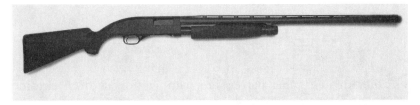

Winchester Model 1300 Black Shadow Field. Winchester's Model 1300 is known for its "speed pump" design. This waterfowling 12 gauge has a 28-inch barrel packed with a modified changeable Win-Choke. A fully floating rib is designed to offer a distortion-free sight plane when the barrel heats from rapid shooting. Smooth pump action with a four-lug rotary bolt system that might make this gun the fastest pump ever. This shotgun's recoil helps you quickly pump another round into the chamber with kinetic force assist. The chamber will handle 2¾- and the bigger 3-inch magnum loads.

Black graphite/composite synthetic forearm and stock with a deluxe recoil pad are virtually indestructible and easy on the body when the shotgun is fired. All outer parts, including the trigger, are a subdued non-glare black matte color. Weighs 7¼ pounds and has a metal bead front sight.

This shotgun is also available in 20 gauge and as a 20 gauge ladies/youth model with more compact stock dimensions. Various camouflaged versions are also available. Contact: U.S. Repeating Arms Co., Dept. NAH, 275 Winchester Ave., New Haven, CT 06511.

3

Non-Toxic, But Deadly

*I*f you take the term "non-toxic" to mean "non-lethal" or "non-deadly," then it's a poor name by which to classify the materials from which shot for waterfowl hunting shotshells is made. The extreme waterfowler wants every shot taken at a duck or goose or swan or crane to be instantly deadly. In the first days of steel shot, there was a legitimate reason to question whether the loads we were mandated to use were indeed "non-lethal".

Under closer scrutiny, the definition for "toxic" only includes illness or damage or death caused by ingestion—eating or drinking—of the substance in question. In the case of waterfowl, it's undeniably proven that birds that pick up too many spent lead pellets while feeding in a hard-bottomed marsh or field are going to suffer some effects, often the fatal effects, of lead poisoning.

How available spent shot is to gritting birds and how long it remains a threat in the environment are still controversial issues among hunters and biologists. However, what frequently surprises even the most extreme waterfowl hunters is how long the idea that spent lead shot in the environment poisons birds and how long the search for acceptable alternatives to lead shot have been around!

Part of bearing the responsibilities of the title "extreme waterfowl hunter" and making the best use of today's non-toxic shot technology is understanding our sport's history and how our equipment was developed. So an historical timeline of the development of non-toxic shot should prove of great interest.

The Development Of Non-Toxic Waterfowling Loads

The history of recognition of lead poisoning in waterfowl species and the ultimate development of non-toxic shot alternatives to lead is long—a lot longer than you might think. This timeline of the development of non-toxic shot was created by compiling information provided by Bill Stevens at Federal Cartridge, Mike Jordan at the Winchester Division of Olin, Mike Prosceno in the press relations office at Remington, the U.S. Fish & Wildlife Service, the Sporting Arms & Ammunition Manufacturer's Institute and a time line of "The History Of The Conversion From Lead Shot To Non-Toxic Shot For Waterfowl Hunting" gathered by renowned non-toxic

Waterfowl that frequent areas with hard bottoms and shallow water are especially susceptible to picking up spent lead pellets.

shot expert Tom Roster for the Cooperative North American Shotgunning Education Program.

1842*—C.J. Fuchs recognized and reported on a lead poisoning problem in waterfowl in Germany.

1874*—The first die-off from lead poisoning in the United States was recognized in Texas.

1918—The U.S. Congress passed the Migratory Bird Treaty Act. This act established federal control of waterfowl seasons, regulations, bag limits and hunting

The greatest problems with lead poisoning were discovered on heavily hunted public areas where frequent shooting was depositing tons of spent shot every season.

methods. More than just waterfowl, the Migratory Bird Treaty Act covers all migratory game birds including doves, woodcock, cranes, coot, rails and other shorebirds. This is the act under which the federal government today has authority to establish seasonal frameworks for the flyways based on which states develop their waterfowl hunting regulations. It is also what allows the federal government to mandate the use of non-toxic shot for hunting of any migratory game bird species.

1919*—Dr. Alexander Wetmore's field observation and controlled experiments conclusively established the link between the ingestion of lead shot by waterfowl and lead poisoning. Wetmore also linked reduced reproductive capacity in birds to sublethal doses of lead.

*Information directly from "The History Of The Conversion From Lead Shot To Non-Toxic Shot For Waterfowl Hunting," copyrighted 1997 by Tom Roster and the Cooperative North American Shotgunning Education Program.

In heavily hunted areas such as the Texas rice country, spent lead shot has built up in the soil profile over the years.

1936—Dr. Dowdell and Dr. Green at the University of Minnesota proposed a lead-magnesium shot material. They indicated this shot would disintegrate in water or the bird's gizzard. The idea was that the shot would break into smaller pieces and not be picked up by birds.

Several unsuccessful attempts were made to produce the shot commercially. In addition, there was no conclusive proof that the lead-magnesium shot was not toxic. In fact, tests in later years proved that the combination was toxic. Discussion and correspondence on lead-magnesium shot continued until 1952.

1948—James Jordan and Frank Bellrose began their research on lead poisoning of ducks. The result of this work was the publication "Lead Poisoning in Wild Waterfowl," Illinois Natural Historical Survey Biological Notes 26, December, 1951. This was one of the first major publications on lead poisoning of ducks.

1949—Additional studies by Bellrose underway.

1950-51—Tested iron shot as a substitute for lead in waterfowl hunting loads.

1959—Frank Bellrose published "Lead Poisoning as a Mortality Factor in Waterfowl Populations" which reported on studies begun in 1949. In this publication, it was estimated that between two and three percent of waterfowl population was lost annually due to lead poisoning. This put the number of ducks lost at approximately two million birds per year! In addition to the information on lead poisoning, data was presented for the first time on the 1950-51 iron-lead shot shooting tests.

1960-1965—Actually beginning in the fall of 1959 and running through the 1966 portion of the 1965 season, estimated annual duck harvests fell below ten million birds. Most of the reduced harvest was because of poor nesting conditions, decreased production and shortened seasons. In addition, the early 1960s were a time when the public developed a greater environmental awareness. All of these things worked together to spur the move to prevent losses of additional waterfowl from spent shot lead poisoning.

1964—The Mississippi Flyway Council prepared a publication on lead poisoning entitled "Wasted Waterfowl." This was a nationwide review of lead poisoning incidents and recommended that a substitute for lead shot be found. In addition, the report contained a review of a 1964-65 lead-iron shot shooting test and a summary of studies conducted on mallards being dosed with lead, lead-coated tin, copper, lead-magnesium and iron shot.

1965—Staff of the Bureau of Sport Fisheries and Wildlife (BSFW) (now the US Fish & Wildlife Service, or USFWS) met with members of the Sporting Arms and Ammunition Manufacturers' Institute (SAAMI) to discuss lead poisoning and the development of a non-toxic shot for waterfowl hunting. This was the first ever meeting which led to the ultimate cooperation between the ammunition industry and Fish & Wildlife agencies to develop steel shot.

1966—Work began on the development of non-toxic shot that was economically feasible and environmentally safe.

1969—On September 19, SAAMI issued the following news release. It provides a comprehensive summary of the dedicated research effort which ultimately pointed to steel shot as the best immediate alternative to lead.

Super-Soft Iron May Solve Lead Poisoning Problems

New York, NY—In late 1966, the director and associate director of the U.S. Bureau of Sport Fisheries and Wildlife (BSFW) informed the leading American and Canadian makers of sporting firearms and ammunition that waterfowl losses caused by lead poisoning might halt duck hunting seasons or force reductions in bag limits on certain flyways. Dabbling ducks ingest spent shot picked up from marsh and feeding ground bottoms. Lead pellets in waterfowl gizzards generate toxic fluids that cause debilitation resulting in starvation or loss through predation.

Lead is universally recognized as the ideal element for shot in sporting ammunition. No other metal or compound offers matching physical or ballistic characteristics, with the exception of gold, silver and certain few other precious metals. Nothing comes close to lead in terms of economy, availability, and product simplicity. Yet lead's toxicity, when ingested by waterfowl, threatens to limit waterfowl hunting as a favorite recreational pursuit enjoyed by millions of American sportsmen.

Responding to the problem, the ammunition and firearms producers through their trade association, SAAMI, began a research program to identify a non-toxic modification or substitute for lead in shotshells for waterfowl hunting.

After careful review of proposals by three organizations known for expertise in the fields of metallurgy, physical ballistics and chemistry, the Illinois Institute of Technology —Research Institute was selected to conduct a 2-year research project. The National Wildlife Research Center at Patuxent, Maryland with staff of the BSFW were program cooperators. They furnished biological test facilities and consultation in ecological balance questions.

IIT-RI explored four general areas: 1) bio-chemical additives for lead that might render the metal harmless in waterfowl systems; 2) lead/iron/plastic composites; 3) plated or coated shot; and 4) iron shot.

In an August, 1969 statement, Ralph Andrews, Chief of the Section of Wetland Ecology for the BSFW said, "...the Patuxent Wildlife Research Center of BSFW screened more than 50 proposed materials and combinations of materials to assess possible toxicities. They found that alloying lead with other metals or coating it with plastics or inert metals did not prevent lead poisoning... Shot pellets made from lead powder bound with water soluble adhesive also failed to pass their tests. In short, no way was found to make lead acceptable."

The bio-chemical additive approach had generated early hope and enthusiasm. It fizzled due to severe problems in producing wire from which shot might be made and died when biological tests showed the materials were toxic.

Results of laboratory production efforts and biological testing with lead/iron/plastic composites mirrored those of the bio-chemical tack. The theory was logically acceptable, cutting the amount of lead in a shot pellet, yet keeping a degree of essential density to achieve desired performance. But it simply did not work in practice.

Iron as a material for shot is not new. It is readily available and low in cost, provided you accept uncontrollable variations and countless non-round globs in the batch. Both defects, added to iron's relatively low density, produce poor ballistic performance in shotshells for waterfowling. This deficiency is compounded by the fact iron shot will erode or "scar" gun barrels and deform chokes. This wear and tear cannot be overcome by coating or plating iron shot with lead or other metals, nor with a variety of plastic shot wrappers or containing wads.

But IIT-RI research efforts have found super-soft iron wire and ways to process the material to assure no adverse effects on gun chokes and barrels. The same research found in mid-1969 that there apparently is no practical mass production method for spherical iron shot.

Are there ballistic deficiencies in soft iron shot? Every duck hunter knows it takes a fair degree of skill plus luck to bring birds to bag, whether decoyed or jump shot or in pass shooting. Can a less dense metal than lead give killing shots? Does it?

"Mortality efficiency" tests were conducted at Patuxent Wildlife Research Center. More than 2,000 pen-raised ducks were sacrificed in a shooting test using "hand-made" soft iron shot in loads equivalent to today's most popular shotshells with lead. The set-up gave bird approach angles exactly as in a true waterfowl hunting situation. Electro-mechanical controls eliminated possibilities for human error or misjudged ranges and aiming leads.

Test results satisfy the experts that shotshells with 1-ounce #4 soft iron shot give almost identical "killing effectiveness" as comparable lead loads when "in-range" shots not exceeding 50 yards are made. In terms of shot-crippled birds, the tests produced results indicating no appreciable difference between soft iron shotshells and comparable lead loads. Evaluation of available data is continuing. A final technical report is planned for issue in the next few months.

Based upon this research and its findings, SAAMI has engaged IIT-RI to develop an economical process for the fabrication of soft iron shot. Indications are their efforts will be successful, according to IIT-RI's Dr. Tom Watmough. Meanwhile, several ammunition producers are independently searching for iron shot production methods and potential suppliers.

While an economically acceptable and ballistically efficient soft iron suitable for waterfowling uses is on the horizon, American sportsmen and conservationists need to understand such shot is not actually in hand. The leading ammunition makers in North America are doing all possible to hasten the advent of iron shot for duck and goose hunting and have every reasonable hope it will eventually be available for loading.

However, when iron shot is introduced for waterfowl hunting, it does nothing to eliminate the tons of lead shot presently on the bottoms of marsh and feeding areas where waterfowl have been hunted over the past half century. Some marsh beds do "turn over"; others remain dormant. Iron shot does not automatically eliminate the exposure that dabbling ducks and feeding geese will experience in many places to available lead pellets. Likewise, the nation's waterfowl hunters must be reminded that acceptance and use of iron shot and its successful substitution for lead in duck loads depends upon the individual hunter's awareness of the true facts in the waterfowl lead poisoning problem and his willingness to do his sportsmanlike share to serve the broad interests of wildlife and natural resources conservation.

1970—As a result of the 1969 report, the International Association of Game, Fish, and Conservation Commissioners (IAGFCC) recommended unanimously that the BSFW take "immediate steps" to "bring about an orderly transition from the use of toxic to nontoxic shot for all hunting of migratory birds" and that "absent a compelling reason by the industry," regulations prohibiting toxic shot should be in place by the 1973 waterfowl season.

Far from looking for excuses not to switch to steel, the ammunition makers were running with the IIT-RI recommendations and working on the formulation of acceptable loads. To do this, research was intensely being conducted to determine proper powders, wads, hulls and primers to create safe, effective steel shot loads. Choke configuration and barrel tolerance studies were also underway.

1972—For the first time, the National Wildlife Federation (NWF) officially took a stance as a major proponent of steel shot regulations

for waterfowl hunting. They petitioned the Department of the Interior for such regulations.

That fall, steel shot was required for the first time on seven National Wildlife Refuges. Ammunition was provided free of charge to the waterfowl hunters hunting those specified areas by the U.S. Fish and Wildlife Service.

1973 — In addition to specified National Wildlife Refuges, Maryland and Wisconsin obtained steel shotshells for a voluntary test program. The shells were resold to hunters who wanted to try steel shot.

In an effort to collect further information about lead poisoning, wing bones were collected from birds harvested by hunters. These were analyzed for lead content, and it was discovered that there was residual lead build-up in the bones from ingestion of spent lead pellets.

1974 — The draft "Environmental Impact Statement in Proposed Use of Steel Shot for Hunting Waterfowl in the United States" was finished. The statement recommended that steel shotshells be required for waterfowl hunting in the Atlantic Flyway in 1976, the Mississippi Flyway in 1977 and the Central and Pacific Flyways in 1978.

In the meantime, the IAGFCC called for local, not flyway-wide prohibition of the use of lead shot through state and federal cooperation—backing off of its earlier recommendation. As a result the USFWS proposed the use of steel in selected areas of the Atlantic Flyway.

1976 — The final version of the Environmental Impact Statement was published, and the USFWS established regulations requiring steel shot for areas in nine states in the Atlantic Flyway. The areas selected were those of known high lead shot deposits and heavy hunting pressure.

Subsequently, the National Rifle Association filed a lawsuit in United States District Court to stop implementation of a lead shot ban. The judge ruled in favor of the USFWS and the restrictions were put in place for the 1976 season.

This suit was important in that it was the first of many unsuccessful attempts to stop the state and federal agencies from mandating non-toxic shot for waterfowl hunting.

1977—Steel shot zones were expanded in the Atlantic Flyway and established in the Mississippi Flyway. Additionally, the USFWS made public the implementation schedule for non-toxic (steel) shot as proposed in the EIS.

1978—Alaska Senator Ted Stevens authored an amendment which was added to the Department of Interior's Appropriation Bill preventing the U.S. Fish & Wildlife Service from using any of its funds to implement or enforce non-toxic shot regulations. Called the "Stevens Amendment" this left the decision primarily up to the states to accept or reject proposed steel shot regulations. Several states rejected the regulations. However, some states accepted the regulations and continued to establish and expand steel shot zones.

1981—The Muldoon Hunting and Fishing Club brought suit against Texas Parks and Wildlife Department for a restraining order to stop implementation of steel shot zones. The judge ruled in favor of Texas Parks and Wildlife Department. Likewise, lawsuits in South Dakota and New York maintained the state conservation departments' right to establish and enforce non-toxic/steel shot regulations.

This year also saw the first meeting of the Inter-Agency Committee on Non-Toxic Shot Regulations. This group was established by the International Association of Fish and Wildlife Agencies to resolve problems that had been created with the implementation of steel shot zones. Members of the committee were from industry, state fish and wildlife agencies, the USFWS and non-profit conservation organizations.

1982—Court cases took place in Florida, New York and South Dakota to stop implementation of steel shot regulations. State agencies won all three cases.

1985—The National Wildlife Federation filed suit to ban waterfowl hunting in parts of five states where bald eagles were purported to have died of lead poisoning from ingesting pellets taken in while eating hit but unrecovered ducks. The court found for the NWF and cited closure of waterfowl hunting in those areas for the 1985-86 season, unless non-toxic shot regulations were implemented immediately for those areas. The action resulted in designation of many new steel shot zones by the USFWS.

Iowa and Nebraska became the first states to implement statewide bans on the use of lead shot for waterfowl hunting.

The Inter-Agency Committee on Non-Toxic Shot Regulations issued a recommendation that steel shot be required for all waterfowl hunting nationwide. It recommended a phase-in schedule where counties of the highest rate of waterfowl harvest (waterfowl harvested per square mile) would be required to use steel shot first.

The following table shows the committee's recommended implementation schedule:

Counties With Harvest Level of Waterfowl / Square Mile	Year Lead Shot Will Be Prohibited
20 or more	1987-88
15 or more	1988-89
10 or more	1989-90
5 or more	1990-91
< 5	1991-92

1986 —The National Wildlife Federation again took the USFWS to court. Their suit contended that there should be a total ban on the use of lead shot for waterfowl hunting in the United States beginning with the 1987 season.

The court ruled in favor of the USFWS which had proposed its backing of the Inter-Agency Committee's phase-in schedule. This plan had been printed in the final addendum to The Final Environmental Impact Statement—Use of Lead Shot for Hunting Migratory Birds in the United States. This final EIS included a summary of all of the lead-steel shot shooting tests conducted since 1950.

1987—The final court test of the USFWS's ability to mandate the use of steel shot took place in a California case filed by the Pacific Legal Foundation. It challenged the USFWS's authority to close waterfowl hunting in areas where the state refused to implement steel shot regulations. The court ruled again in favor of the USFWS.

As a result of the phase-in of steel shot regulations underway, many states voluntarily went statewide with their lead shot bans to simplify regulations and enforcement.

Hunters can find success with non-toxic shot if they are willing to commit the time to learn to shoot it and understand its limitations.

1990—Provincial governments in Ontario and British Columbia established steel shot zones for implementation in 1991.

1991—With the opening gun of the earliest waterfowl seasons in the US, the phase-in of the lead shot ban was complete. All waterfowl hunting whether over field, marsh or open water, must be done with a USFWS approved non-toxic shot. Lead shot is no longer legal for hunting waterfowl in the United States.

Steel shot zones have been established at Oak Hammock Marsh north of Winnipeg, Manitoba. Geese there were proven to be ingesting spent lead shot in the feeding fields around the management area.

1992—Steel shot zones are established in Nova Scotia and New Brunswick.

1994—The Bismuth Cartridge Company petitioned the USFWS to approve its bismuth-tin compound as a non-toxic shot material for the 1994-95 waterfowl season. Though testing was incomplete, conditional approval was granted on December 30 for the remainder of the 1994-95 season. Any federally approved non-toxic shot automatically becomes legal in some states; others specifically require steel shot by regulation.

Steel shot zones are established in Prince Edward Island and Quebec.

1995—USFWS issued extension of provisional approval of bismuth shot for the 1995-96 waterfowl season. The USFWS also initiated regulations to ban lead shot for all types of scattershot shotgun hunting on National Wildlife Refuges by 1998.

Canada announced its plans for a complete lead shot ban for waterfowl hunting beginning with the 1997 waterfowl season. Its regulations will call for approval of non-toxic shot materials by the Canadian Wildlife Service (CWS).

1996—Federal Cartridge introduced Premium and Classic High Velocity steel loads. This new generation of steel shot load reduces payload in a 12 gauge 3-inch shell from 1¼ ounces to 1⅜ ounces but increases muzzle velocity from 1,375 feet per second (fps) to 1,450 fps. Waterfowlers begin to notice quicker, more efficient kills especially on large birds like geese, swans and cranes.

Federal Cartridge also applied with USFWS and CWS for approval of tungsten-iron shot as a non-toxic waterfowl load. Another conditional approval was also granted for bismuth-tin shot for the 1996-97 season.

1997—USFWS and the CWS granted conditional approval for tungsten-iron shot for the 1997-98 waterfowl season.

Bismuth-tin shot was granted full approval by the USFWS and CWS as a non-toxic load and received the official endorsement of Ducks Unlimited. Additionally, Winchester and Bismuth Cartridge companies announced a techno-

Federal Premium High Velocity Steel shells were introduced in 1996. They caught on quickly, especially with goose, crane and swan hunters.

logical alliance to improve manufacture and distribution of bis-muth-tin loaded non-toxic shotshells.

Winchester also introduced Supreme High Velocity Drylok Super Steel loads which also provide a boost in muzzle velocity from a 3-inch 12 gauge shell to 1,450 feet per second with a 1¼ ounce payload.

Prior to the hunting season, Canada repealed its complete ban on lead shot for waterfowl hunting. Regulations for the 1997 season allowed the use of lead shot for field hunting for at least that season, but required non-toxic shot in areas where pellets were likely to fall

As of the 2000 hunting season, all waterfowl hunting in Canada will require non-toxic shot approved by the Canadian Wild-life Service.

in water. Though anticipated, no announcement has yet been made confirming a total lead shot ban in Canada for 1998 and beyond.

Later in the year, Federal Cartridge applied to USFWS for conditional approval of tungsten-polymer composite as non-toxic shot material for the 1998-99 waterfowl seasons.

Where That Leaves Us

Extreme waterfowl hunters know that the days of lead shot for waterfowl hunting are gone, never to return. Heck, depending on where you do most of your duck and goose hunting, you may very well have been shooting steel shot for more than 20 years already! It won't be long and an entire generation of extreme waterfowl hunters will have been born and launched on their hunting careers never having fired a lead-loaded shell at a duck.

Lead's gone and it's not coming back. In fact, we're likely to see yearly expansion of the requirements for the use of non-toxic shot in upland bird hunting and even target shooting. All of us, extreme and non-extreme waterfowl hunters alike, need to stop mourning over and pining for lead shot for duck hunting.

The extreme waterfowl hunter's time is much better spent researching what is available and learning to maximize its effectiveness in cleanly killing ducks and geese. Despite what the nay-sayers may tell you, selecting from today's non-toxic load options is not a matter of choosing the lesser evil.

We've come a long way from those early days of steel. Today's steel shotshells from Winchester, Remington, Federal, Fiocchi and others are faster, utilize more researched and better designed components and take advantage of new steps in powder technology. They will kill ducks and geese dead if you recognize their limitations and take the time to learn how to use them.

A strong argument can be made that bismuth-tin and tungsten-iron shot is as effective as lead ever was—in some situations perhaps more effective! And the search for even better materials and better ways to load existing materials continues.

Making Your Choice In Waterfowl Loads

Until the next revolution in non-toxic shotshells comes along, today's extreme waterfowl hunter has four choices in selecting the loads he'll use to make clean, instant kills. Three of them can definitely be relied upon to put birds in your bag.

Speed Kills

The high velocity steel loads from Federal, Winchester and Fiocchi are quickly proving the philosophy that speed kills ducks and geese and cranes. The most common complaint with steel shot is wounding or, more precisely, delayed kills. Every hunter who has spent enough time in the blind to consider himself or herself extreme has seen birds hit with steel shot fly out of range seemingly almost uninjured, then fold up stone dead almost out of sight.

It's believed that the reason for that is that steel, being many times harder than lead shot, does not deform and stop inside the bird the way lead would have. Most times, especially in the larger shot sizes, the steel slices cleanly all the way through the bird. Unless pellets hit the spine or break wing bones, the bird takes some time to die.

It's very similar to the difference between the way a high velocity rifle bullet and a broadhead-tipped arrow kill a big game animal. The bullet kills by hydrostatic shock; that is, the sudden transfer of energy from a mushrooming bullet to the central nervous system of the animal. Or like a blow to the head with a sledgehammer. That's why a bullet that mushrooms but stays in one piece is so crucial for clean kills on big game animals.

A properly placed broadhead, on the other hand, slices cleanly through soft tissue, causing hemorrhaging, or bleeding. Its intent is to kill the animal by bleeding to death, so seldom is there "knock down" with a broadhead. Death is quick from severe tissue damage but seldom instantaneous.

So it often is with steel shot. The wounds are mortal, but the birds have to bleed out before they die. Unfortunately, because they are flying across water and incredibly thick terrain, it's seldom possible to visually follow a blood trail to a web-footed trophy. Steel shot has made the hunting partnership with an extreme retriever all the more important.

The high velocity steel loads are helping hunters kill the birds more quickly and closer to the blind. Here's how.

The same steel pellets are hitting the birds, and, obviously because they are moving even faster, they penetrate all the way through just like the lower velocity loads. However, the pellets from the high velocity loads are still traveling faster when they hit the bird. That means their kinetic energy is greater, so they are hitting the birds harder. There's more shock even though the steel is still passing through the bird.

Extreme waterfowl hunters who are sticking with steel, but haven't yet tried high velocity steel shells, owe it to themselves and the birds to use it for a season and judge the results for themselves. They'll be impressed.

The high velocity steel loads (especially in small shot sizes like 6 and 7) make great dove loads, and hunting doves with them is an outstanding way to learn to shoot the shells well.

Steel Shot Size Selection

In the nearly 20 years that it took to phase-in steel shot, extreme waterfowlers have heard it 10,000 times if they've heard it once. The advice from the ammo makers and the experts has been when selecting shot size for your steel waterfowl loads, jump up two sizes from your favorite lead load to achieve similar performance.

Today that advice is antiquated. There are many waterfowl hunters who never had a favorite lead waterfowl load because they have never hunted waterfowl with lead! So for today's waterfowlers, here's some recommended starting points from one extreme waterfowler to others. And by the way, these recommendations are based on shooting 12 gauge 2¾ or 3-inch magnums. You can feel confident in using the largest shot sizes in the 10 gauge or 12 gauge 3½-inch magnums, because with the added payload of shot, you'll get plenty of pellet strikes even on the smaller birds.

Hunting Situation	Recommended Shot Sizes
Early-season ducks over decoys (teal, woodies)	#3, #4
Mallards & divers over decoys	#2
Pass-shooting ducks	BB, #1
Jump-shooting ducks	#2
Sea ducks	BB, #1
Large geese (greater and giant Canadas)	BBB, T
Medium and small geese (specks, snows, etc.)	BBB

When in doubt with steel shot, go to the larger shot sizes (that is, if you are using a modern firearm with a barrel and chokes approved for steel shot, and if you're willing to find a choke/load combination that patterns well from your favored hunting rig).

Advantages To Steel?

Most of the time, circles of old-time extreme waterfowlers only talk about the blemishes on steel shot's reputation. You've heard it: "...sure doesn't kill the way lead did."

No, it doesn't kill on target the way lead used to, nor does it kill for years afterward laying on the bottom of a shallow slough! Used within its limitations by a smart, conscientious extreme waterfowl hunter, steel can kill very effectively.

The main limitation is range. However, the

Medium-sized waterfowl, like this specklebelly, can be taken cleanly to 40 yards with high velocity steel shells in shot sizes like BB and BBB.

extreme waterfowler doesn't view that so much as a limitation but more like an added challenge. After all, the allure of extreme waterfowling is using all of one's hunting skills to bring the birds close and closer! Waterfowlers could take a lesson from turkey hunters who frequently brag of taking birds at ten yards and closer! Steel, especially high velocity steel, has all it takes to kill well-shot birds cleanly, up to and including the size of a tundra swan, out to 30 yards. If we've done it all right, we shouldn't need to shoot farther than that anyway!

Though it can be as effective, shooting steel is undeniably different from shooting lead. Even somebody who shoots thousands of clay targets in the "off season" (though that really doesn't exist for the extreme waterfowl hunter) with lead loads can't expect to load up with steel on opening day and be fully on his or her game!

Shooting practice is important. Shooting more and shooting more often, even with standard lead target loads at 1,100 to 1,200 feet per second, will help entrench good shooting basics. However, it must be remembered that the ballistics of steel loads are different from lead.

First of all, even standard velocity 2¾-inch 12 gauge magnum steel loads start out of the muzzle at a minimum of 1,300 feet per second, usually 1,350 or higher. So at close ranges you need to lead the bird less with steel. Because the individual pellets of steel are lighter than pellets of lead of the same diameter, they lose energy and slow down faster, meaning that at longer range more lead is required.

There are several ways to shoot better in the waterfowl blind come opening day. One is to find a sporting clays course that will let you shoot full-power steel field loads and shoot a couple of rounds to "get the feel back" before season opens. Another is to shoot the latter part of the practice season with steel target loads. Remington and Winchester both produce factory loaded target rounds with steel shot in sizes, velocities and recoil more appropriate to clay birds. If you're fortunate enough to get in some dove hunting prior to the waterfowl season, give these steel target loads a try! They run about 1,250 fps muzzle velocity and are deadly on doves that seem adept at getting out of the way of standard velocity lead loads.

You can always go to the blind and tune in shooting steel during the season, but make it your mantra each time your finger twitches toward the safety, "Closer, faster, closer, faster...now!"

Though in field performance steel will have to take a back seat to bismuth-tin shot and to tungsten-iron shot, it will continue to be the mainstay of waterfowl hunters everywhere because of its greatest advantage. Steel loads will always be less expensive than bismuth, tungsten or any other proprietary shot material that's likely to come down the pike. Steel is likely to continue at half the price or less of the high-tech alternatives.

If you shoot enough waterfowl loads during the course of a season to make price a major consideration, fear not. The top-shelf steel loads coming out of the factory gates can and will get the job done for you.

Bismuth: As Close To Lead As You Can Get

Bismuth is an element that lies next to lead on the periodic table. It's similar to lead in density, making it heavier and softer than steel, therefore ballistically superior to steel. Bismuth is found in deposits with tin, copper, tungsten, gold, silver and lead. It's separated from the ore and the other metals during the refining process.

To make a metal suitable for the production of shot pellets, bismuth is alloyed to tin. The ratio is 97 percent bismuth and

Bismuth shells can account for a truly mixed bag even from older guns with barrel walls too thin to shoot steel or tungsten loads.

3 percent tin. Tin is added to the bismuth to soften the shot a little bit. Pure bismuth shot shatters too easily under the forces of firing and traveling down a shotgun barrel.

That "frangibility" or likeliness for pellets to shear apart was one of the early criticisms leveled at bismuth shot, but refinements of the mix and production methods have pretty much eliminated that problem. Today, independent tests have indicated that loss due to all causes (deformation, flyers, breakage, etc.) in properly loaded bismuth shells is less than two percent. Two percent pellet loss is also encountered with equivalent lead loads due to flyers, which are deformed pellets that fly erratically and leave the pattern before it reaches its target. Since bismuth shotshells are loaded by weight, any given bismuth load will contain more pellets than the comparable (by weight) lead load. So the pattern will actually contain more pellets when it reaches the target, thus increasing the chances of pellet strikes and energy transfer to the target!

Bismuth-tin shot was first granted conditional approval as a non-toxic shot for waterfowl hunting by the USFWS late in 1994. It was in time to catch the tail end of the 1994-95 waterfowl season, but distribution of the shot was limited, so it wasn't available for very many hunters to try. Conditional approval was extended for the 1995-96 season and again for the 1996-1997 season. In 1997 it was granted full approval by the USFWS, making it the only market-proven "heavy metal" shot material proven non-toxic and non-carcinogenic.

Bismuth-tin shot was originally developed, loaded and marketed by the Bismuth Cartridge Company under the No-Tox trademark. In 1997, a technological alliance was formed with Winchester Ammunition. The bismuth loaded shells now available are loaded using proven Winchester components and production processes.

What makes the bismuth-tin a great non-toxic shot substitute for lead is the fact that its performance is so close to that of

lead. First off, that makes it easy to switch from your inexpensive lead practice loads in the mock blind on the sporting clays course to the non-toxic substitute on opening day without having to change your hard-earned leads and your shooting style. There's no tune-in time like there is with the higher velocity, ballistically inferior steel loads.

Bismuth is more expensive than high velocity steel but can "save the day" for extreme waterfowl hunters when conditions are the toughest!

Bismuth loaded shotshells are a godsend to extreme waterfowlers for whom a big part of the experience of waterfowling is shooting his or her birds with a fine old shotgun. Bismuth shot is by far the softest of the non-toxic alternatives to lead. Therefore it can be loaded much like lead was and is safe to use even in an old side-by-side with thin barrel walls as long as it is proofed safe for full-power, smokeless powder lead loads. In fact, it's the only non-toxic shot that is recommended by Purdey & Sons and Holland & Holland for use in their fine, custom-built guns.

Choke selection is also similar to those you'd make when using lead shot. Depending on ranges and conditions, bismuth shot will perform well and safely in chokes from cylinder bore to extra-full. There is no danger to shotguns with interchangeable choke tubes marked for lead only, or old guns. Of course, no modern smokeless powder load is meant for use in shotguns with Damascus or twist steel barrels.

Because of its similarity to lead, bismuth is also loaded by the Bismuth Cartridge/Winchester ammunition alliance in the full range of gauges from 10 to .410 cal. There are even 2½-inch shells in 12 gauge and .410 cal. for fine old European guns with shorter chambers. While the lighter loads are more suitable to upland bird hunting in the growing number of areas requiring non-toxic shot for that pursuit, extreme waterfowlers will be most interested in Bismuth's Magnum Buffered Game Loads offered in 10 gauge, 12 gauge 3½-inch, 12 gauge 3-inch and 12 gauge 2¾-inch. Shot sizes in these loads range from BB to 6, so if you had a favorite lead load you can come close to matching it with bismuth. In case you didn't, here are some recommendations for starters:

Hunting Situation	Recommended Shot Sizes
Early season ducks over decoys (teal, woodies)	#6, #5
Mallards & divers over decoys	#4
Pass-shooting ducks	#2, #4
Jump-shooting ducks	#5
Sea ducks	#2
Large geese (greater and giant Canadas)	BB
Medium and small geese (specks, snows, etc.)	BB, #2

The greatest drawback, perhaps the only drawback, to shooting bismuth shells is price. In the loads of interest to the extreme waterfowl hunter, the shells are about double the price of top-shelf, high velocity steel loads. Every time you drop the firing pin on the

For those of slighter build who need to shoot 20 gauge guns, bismuth shells are the far superior selection.

primer of a standard 12 gauge bismuth shell, it's going to cost you well over $1.00. And unlike other consumer products in which prices drop as technology advances, that's not likely to be the case with bismuth-tin loaded shells. Extraction costs and processing costs to convert the raw material to useable product are much higher than steel or lead. And the Bismuth Cartridge Company owns the market as far as bismuth's use in shot is concerned.

For the hunter who only makes it to the blind a half-dozen times per season and shoots just a few boxes of shells, the added expense won't mean much and he'll do well to load up with bismuth. But for the extreme among us who spend perhaps 60, 70 or even a 100 days a year in the blind and use cases of shells, bismuth and other proprietary non-toxic shot cartridges will probably only see specialized use when conditions are at their toughest—the way we like them!

Tungsten Reaches New Heights

Compared to where we're at now, the first steel shells were poor. Concentrated research by all of the ammo makers resulted in more consistent shot, drastically improved shot cups, better waterproofing and, most recently, higher velocities. All of this means more powerful, more consistent loads. Today's steel shot loads are mighty good. Used within their limits, they are fine hunting loads.

Federal's new Premium Tungsten load is better than steel. A lot better! And though this extreme waterfowl hunter is going by recollections nearly 20 years old (that's how long it's been since I hunted waterfowl regularly with lead shot), tungsten-iron shot may prove itself as good or better than lead ever was!

By way of a field test before tungsten received its conditional approval from the USFWS, Federal gathered a crew of shotgunning writers and editors at Bittern Lake Lodge, not far from Edmonton, Alberta in the fall of 1996. The assignment was to shoot our limits of ducks and geese using as many, or as few, tungsten loaded shells as deemed necessary.

The ducks cooperated. I've enjoyed several hunts in Canada and the United States that certainly must compare to "the good old days;" I've never seen anything like the Alberta Parklands in the fall of 1996. Shooting a limit of eight greenheads was downright easy, most any time of day!

One afternoon, NAHC Shooting Advisory Council Member Nick Sisley, *Outdoor Life* Shooting Editor Jim Carmichel and I were assigned to a grain field on a small ridge above a cattle pasture with a couple of slough holes in the middle of it. Our guide spaced us along the fenceline between these fields and placed a dozen black silhouette duck cut-outs nearly at the crest of the ridge. He then took up a position at the fence corner.

I had flown my top Lab, Sadie, along for the early-season work, and the guide had his male Lab. We figured it would be a great chance to polish their honoring. Besides, fetching up 32 ducks in two hours for a line of gunners a quarter-mile long is a lot to ask of one dog—especially one that had already hunted that morning!

Walking in, Nick and Jim and I agreed that with the great shoot we were expecting from these dry and comfortable hides, this would be the best "field test" of the tungsten. We also decided that because this truly needed to be a test, we'd take no ducks closer than 35 yards and, depending on the shot presented, we might try to reach out to 70 yards. (Again, this was a test. Extreme waterfowling is about getting the birds in close!)

Federal's Tungsten-Iron shells are fast and hit hard. The shot is actually a combination of tungsten and iron.

We took our 32 ducks in a couple hours. The dogs picked up all the ducks shot. Not one was lost. Only two birds came in with their heads up; the rest were stone dead. When hit with the tungsten shot, they folded instantly the way you might remember way back in the days of lead shot.

On the previous hunts during the trip, I had trouble hitting consistently with the tungsten, particularly at longer ranges. I finally determined the problem was that I was shooting ahead of the birds. That's right, ahead of the birds at maximum ranges!

Having shot steel for so long, my natural reaction to missing on the first shot was to pull farther ahead and slap the trigger again. To hit with tungsten, I found that I had to reduce my lead! For anyone used to shooting a lot of lead at the sporting clays course, it feels odd allowing the duck to catch up to the bead at 50 yards!

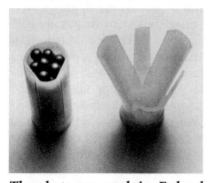

The shot cup used in Federal Tungsten-iron shotshells protects the barrel from the extremely hard shot.

Federal's tungsten shot is actually made from 60 percent iron and 40 percent tungsten. The resulting material is 32 percent denser than steel and 94 percent as dense as lead! Factory reported velocity on the 3-inch 1⅛-ounce loads we were shooting is 1,400 fps. Because the per-pellet weight is greater than steel yet launched at approximately the same velocity as the fastest steel loads, it retains more speed and energy per pellet to greater ranges. Thus, required lead is the same up close but less at maximum ranges.

Though a third more dense than steel, tungsten-iron shot is even harder than steel used in either shot or in the manufacture of shotgun barrels, so you can rest assured that there's no deformation of firing or on target. While this means that all of the pellets will stay in the pattern, it does present some problems. First is potential barrel and choke damage from shot that's actually harder than the barrel.

The barrel is protected by Federal's patented wad design, which incorporates six overlapping petals. The wad is built sort of like nature created the artichoke. The artichoke's leaves are in concentric layers, each layer's leaves overlapping dead center on the meeting point of the leaves of the next layer in. On the Federal wad, there are three inner petals overlapped by three outer petals.

This design offers double-layer protection of the barrel walls from passing shot and vice versa. On exiting the muzzle, the petals open and catch air quickly, leaving the pattern to fly on its own in very short order. The faster the separation of the wad from the shot after the load leaves the barrel, the better the performance of the pattern.

The wad in Federal's tungsten-iron shells is heavy and thick. It has to be to do its job. Yet that also means that it takes up a great deal of the finite space inside the hull. As a result, the payload of shot in a 12 gauge 3-inch magnum Federal Premium Tungsten load is only 1⅛ ounces of shot. In pure pellet count that's substantially fewer than steel or bismuth loads based on the same pellets of the same shot size in a comparable load.

Yet that reduced overall payload weight does offer one advantage. It allows tungsten pellets to be cranked out of the muzzle at 1,400 fps in the 12 gauge 3-inch magnum and 1,450 fps in the 2¾-inch magnum! And because tungsten-iron shot is denser that any of the other non-toxic shot materials (meaning that individual pellets of tungsten weigh more) they carry more energy to greater distances. So in comparison, the overall payload in a bismuth shell has more energy because its total weight is heavier. But on a per pellet basis, the faster flying, heavier tungsten-iron shot carries more energy to the target.

The extreme waterfowler is as familiar with this conundrum as with "which came first, the chicken or the egg?" Is it better to hit a duck or goose with more pellets carrying less energy per pellet or fewer pellets carrying more energy per pellet? For the extreme water-fowler, the decision must be based on the results you get at the patterning board and finally in the field!

Tungsten-iron loads should not be fired from any shotgun or choke from which you wouldn't fire lead shot. Tungsten loads pattern tightly! I tried shooting it in an old, tightly choked Remington 870 with poor results. The choke was simply too tight.

The day of that first field test, I was using a modified Remchoke in my Remington 11-87 Special Purpose, which is what Jim also had in the 870 he was shooting. I think the tubes in Nick's over/under were a strong improved and a weak modified. In your pattern testing, begin with skeet 1 and work up to modified if you deem it necessary. Tighter than that will likely be counterproductive.

In the States, tungsten-iron shot received conditional approval from the USFWS for use during the 1997-98 season, which will likely be extended for upcoming seasons until it ultimately receives full approval. It has also received approval from the Canadian Wildlife Service.

Selecting shot sizes for tungsten loads, at least for the time being, is a simple matter. Only sizes #2 and BB are available. Stick with the #2s for big ducks and small geese. Use BB for big geese, cranes and swans.

As exciting as the prospects of this "better than lead" load are, there is one drawback. You might have guessed; it's the price!

A box of ten Federal Premium Tungsten shells will cost you almost $20. Yep, that's nearly $2 a shell.

For the amount of shells the extreme waterfowl hunter shoots chasing ducks and geese and cranes from Canada to the Gulf of Mexico each year, that's simply too much to make them everyday shells. However, there should be a place in every extreme water-fowler's bag of tricks for this high-price ammo.

These geese were taken in the early 1980s in Wisconsin's famed Horicon Marsh area, which has required non-toxic shot since the late 1970s! Today's non-toxic shotshell choices are far superior.

Perhaps you'll start each day's hunt with my favorite high velocity steel shells in good supply. During the first one to two hours, judge how the birds are working. If everything is right, and they're landing on top of you like they should be, stick with the steel. If the birds are showing no interest and staying well out of range, stick with the steel.

But if it turns out to be one of those days when the birds are looking you over, yet flock after flock peels back at 45-50 yards no matter what you try, then break out the tungsten and have at 'em. It's got the same velocity as your high speed steel, so swing and leads will be much the same!

The Next Generation Of Tungsten

There are problems with tungsten-iron shot. Because of its hardness many times greater than lead or bismuth, it requires that thick, space-eating wad shotcup. In gauges smaller than 12, it couldn't be loaded in sufficient quantity to be practical—the wad would take up more space than the shot! On top of that, tungsten-iron is difficult, if not impossible, to manufacture in shot sizes smaller than #4. That pretty much limits its usefulness to waterfowl hunting.

To overcome these problems, Federal has developed tungsten-polymer shot and has applied for conditional approval of the composite material as an accepted non-toxic shot from the USFWS and the CWS. Federal touts the new loads as having the same velocity of steel and the pellet energy of lead, and as being safe for all types of firearms proofed for smokeless loads.

Initial offerings of Federal Premium Tungsten/Polymer loads will be in 12 gauge 2¾- and 3-inch with sizes #4 and #6 shot.

4

Wingshooting For
Waterfowl Hunters

*A*s far as guns go, there's no question that the extreme waterfowl
hunters of the 21st century are better equipped to cleanly, humanely
harvest their game than any of the hunters who waded the marshes
or squinted to see through pit blind covers before them.
Ammunition did become a disadvantage for awhile, but extreme
waterfowl hunters and the ammo makers now have more than 20
years of experience with steel under their wader belts. On top of that,
the latest non-toxic shot materials are coming mighty close to
accomplishing our objectives the way lead used to.

Yet the finest, most reliable shotgun loaded with state-of-the-
science shotshells is only as good as the hunter behind it. The true
extreme waterfowler takes pride in his wingshooting skills. And
waterfowling wingshooting skills are earned only one way. Through
practice, practice and more practice.

Though the extreme waterfowl hunters who will see the turn of
the next century carry better shotguns and load highly-refined shotshells, the hunters at the turn of the last century had a big leg up on
us when it came to honing their waterfowling wingshooting skills.
Duck season was longer and bag limits were higher or nonexistent!
They could become great duck shots by shooting at ducks.

That can't happen today and will never happen again. Now, the extreme waterfowl hunter must learn wingshooting skills on the clay target range. And once they are learned, he or she must develop a practice regimen that will translate those skills directly to the blind from sunrise on opening day through sunset on closing day.

Perhaps that sounds a lot harder than it actually is. Heck, remember that waterfowl hunting is a lifestyle, a year-round pursuit for the extreme waterfowl hunter. If you wear that rank proudly, then you're constantly on the lookout for ways to connect the off-season days to in-season days. Shooting at clay targets with the specified purpose of making yourself a better duck shot is a great connection— and better yet, it's fun.

Getting The Right Start

There are many ways to learn to shoot a shotgun. Most of us probably take the most difficult route, which is to head for the hills with family or friends with a case of clay targets, some shells and a target thrower of some kind. That's fun, but it's almost a certain way to pick up bad habits that will have to be overcome later on to really fine-tune your skills. If you don't agree, think back to the first times you went shotgunning. Were you told to shoot with one eye closed? Were you allowed to load more than one shell at a time? Were you told to "keep shooting 'til you hit something?" Were you allowed to shoot until you felt so tired you could barely lift the gun?

All of those common occurrences in backyard shooting can create bad habits in a beginning shooter that will take hundreds of targets and perhaps even more dollars to correct later on.

The best way for a beginner to learn shotgunning would be to take lessons with a qualified, professional instructor from day one. Perhaps it's because hunting is the ultimate generational sport— father teaches son—but hunters are way behind the curve on seeking professional instruction to learn and improve shooting skills. In sports like golf, tennis and skiing, professional instruction of beginners and advanced coaching for veterans has always been the way solid skills are developed and improved upon.

Since hunting is the ultimate extreme sport, compare it to skydiving. There isn't anyone who jumps out of a perfectly good airplane without receiving expert instruction!

Waterfowlers face especially challenging wingshooting situations like shooting while sitting or even lying down.

Professional shooting instruction is more available and closer to home than you might think. Most sporting clays courses, which now number in the thousands across the United States, have a "pro" who is available for shooting lessons and who can tailor his or her instruction to shooters of any skill level. And they can spot bad habits faster than an extreme waterfowl hunter can spot a band on a bird's leg!

On top of that, shooting schools run by firearms and ammunition manufacturers as well as private instructors are cropping up all over the country. Some of them travel all over, and arrangements can be made for them to come to you. The reference list at the end of this chapter will provide some places to begin your search.

Shooting lessons are not inexpensive, but they are well worth the investment for anyone serious about improving his or her waterfowling wingshooting skills.

The next best way to learn is with the assistance of good books and videos. There are many available, and you can find them at the library and local video stores if you want to "field test" them before you buy them!

Successful wingshooting for the extreme waterfowler begins here—on the sporting clays range with a good coach!

One complete wingshooting course that can create superb shooting skills in a beginner and can sharpen the eye of the most veteran extreme waterfowl hunter is called "Shoot Where You Look," and it was developed by North American Hunting Club Life Member Leon Measures.

Shoot Where You Look

Despite starting with a BB gun shooting at a stationary target, the "Shoot Where You Look" program can help improve any eager student's wingshooting skills from first-time shooter to class AA competitive shooter. Even an extreme waterfowl hunter can benefit from this multimedia shooting course.

The chance for me to meet "Shoot Where You Look" creator Leon Measures came while taping "North American Outdoors" for ESPN. The production schedule was mighty tight, so ours was a one-day crash-course touching only briefly on the basics of Leon's program. But even in that short time, Leon had me consistently hitting hand-tossed pennies with a BB gun. That's right—a BB gun.

A special, sightless Daisy BB gun is the basis for Leon's program. With it and his firm but gentle guidance, Leon can teach anyone with decent eyesight to hit hand-tossed aspirin out of the air after two weeks of training. Most of his students are kids who have never shot a gun of any type before!

And get this: while we were there with the television cameras running, a couple of Leon's third session students learned to hit hand thrown BBs out of the air with a BB gun. That's right, hitting one BB with another one. Had I not seen it, I never would have believed it.

Leon takes a penny or a dime the student has just shot out of the air and finds the dent in the coin. He takes another BB and lays it in the dent. Then he asks the student, what would have happened if that point on the coin had been a BB? "Well, I would have hit it," says the student.

Leon says, "Then let's do it." And most of them do in the first couple tries and frequently thereafter. It proves one of the basic theories of the "Shoot Where You Look" program—the center of every target is exactly the same size.

That's one of the most important lessons of the "Shoot Where You Look" program for extreme waterfowl hunters to learn. The center of every target is exactly the same size. Big birds in particular seem to give waterfowl hunters fits. If you look up there at a goose or a swan or a crane and you think "I can't miss that thing," then you are definitely missing the point. Whether the feathered fowl is a 10-ounce teal or a 20-pound tundra swan, the center of the target—the spot you need to be looking at—is exactly the same size!

Some bowhunters put decals on the back of the upper limb of their bows. The words on the stickers read "Pick A Spot." That's exactly what you should do on a bird. Pick a spot, like the goose's eye or the point of the pintail's bill, and focus on that spot. Don't aim, because you point a shotgun, you do not aim a shotgun. *Look* at that spot. When you do, every bird you're shooting at becomes exactly the same size. It will end any problems you might have about thinking larger birds are moving slower than they really are. And by picking a spot at the very front end of the bird, you're concentrating on the most vital area—the head and neck! By making this principle part of your wingshooting instinct, you'll find yourself calling head shots on ducks as small as teal before your retriever puts them in your hand!

Another crucial concept of "Shoot Where You Look" is beginning your swing before your shotgun ever comes up. As Leon teaches from day one of the course, when the gun hits your shoulder you should be firing. If you don't you'll miss. It's what you might call the "just shoot it" principle.

Never was the "just shoot it" principle made more clear to me than on a recent hunt in Central California's Sink Butte area. My hunting companions were Mike Jordan (the extreme waterfowl hunter who has been with Winchester for more than 30 years, not the guy who plays extreme basketball) and Ron Stromstad, another extreme waterfowler who just happens to be Director of Operations for Ducks Unlimited's Western Regional Office. By the luck of a special invitation we were experiencing a windy day on the area's premier private duck club. It was a once in a lifetime chance to add a once in a lifetime experience to each of our extreme collections.

While the wind kept the birds on the wing, it also made shooting interesting. Ducks working, then landing into the wind seemed to be hovering, not moving at all. That led to me missing some "easy" first shots because I believed my eyes instead of my instincts. Second shots were at birds at least 15 yards farther away as they peeled back into the wind. Ducks going past the blind with the wind just got a chuckle from all of us as we marveled at the greenwings going Mach 2.

That is, until I caught a glimpse of a drake rocketing over my end of the blind. Almost without thinking, I pulled up and shot that duck dead as a hammer. When Ron handed me the bird a moment later, all he said was "head shot."

Later on, as we marveled over our bag of pintails, mallards and greenwing teal, I had to admit that the speeding teal had seemed like the easiest shot all morning. I missed big ducks landing into the wind because I would watch them forever, trying to guess how fast they'd be going, estimating leads, swinging and second guessing ... planning my shots. The tiny teal was taken by true instinctive shooting. When the gun hit my shoulder it went off and the teal came down. That's the very definition of shooting where you look.

The "Shoot Where You Look" program has led thousands of shooters young and old, novice and veteran, to improve their wing-shooting skills. The program is available as a complete package including the sightless Daisy BB gun with cross-bolt safety, 2,000 BBs, comprehensive video, complete guidebook/workbook, two pairs of safety glasses, a shoulder patch and UPS delivery anywhere in the 48 states. Total package cost is $165. I'll give you an address to get hold of Leon at the end of this chapter.

Because of the BB guns, Leon's program may sound like it's exclusively for youngsters or beginning shooters. It's not! You can undertake the video course seriously in your own basement during the "off season." It will do a lot to smooth out the hitches in any wingshooter's swing and will enhance your concentration skills.

You're far better off to spend a few dollars to get started on the right foot with this program for wingshooters.

Practice With A Purpose

Practice makes perfect. Shotgunners of every stature have been preached that doctrine a million times. Now make it a million and one. They, in turn, preach it to friends and acquaintances approaching the realm of extreme waterfowl hunter. And the vicious cycle goes on and on.

In some cases though, it might be closer to the truth to say practice can be pointless. It can, if the practice sessions are without purpose. To walk out on a field and shoot a shotgun into the sky is not practice. Even the addition of targets flying about does not necessarily constitute legitimate practice.

Practice in developing and sharpening waterfowling wingshooting skills, as in anything else, is only worth the effort if you concentrate on what you are doing—really concentrate. To achieve progress, each practice session and each practice target must have a specific purpose. Have a plan of what you're trying to learn.

Critique each target shot. Think it through. Where did you miss that target? Why did you miss it? What can you do on the next shot to hit it? But don't just concentrate on the negatives. Go through the same routine when you break a target. Again, think it through. What made that shot feel right? Where was the barrel when you began your swing? Where was it in relation to the target when you pulled the trigger? What did the follow-through feel like? Try to imprint those sights and sensations on your brain and use them to hit other targets at the range and, more importantly, in the blind.

Once you've mastered the basics, take every opportunity to try new things to test your skills. Maybe it's doubles from station four on the skeet field. Maybe it's trap targets while standing on top of the house or in the bleachers behind the field. Try to come up with ways to duplicate shots that you'll see from the blind and practice them in "reps" like a weightlifter pumps iron in the gym. Once a particular shot has been engraved in your memory banks, it's difficult to wipe out, even if it is practiced only occasionally after that.

At this stage in a wingshooter's development, a qualified coach can be a huge help. He or she can pick up on what you're doing wrong and doing right and explain to you when you don't have a clue as to why you're missing one particular kind of shot and nailing another.

This is also the time at which those informal shooting sessions with friends and a portable trap can be beneficial. If you're careful, you'll be beyond deeply instilling too many bad habits.

Mastering Waterfowling's Toughest Shot

Ask any bunch of wingshooters what they consider the most difficult shot to hit consistently. You'll likely get a variety of answers until one of the gang mentions the falling or dropping target. In a split second, the rest will be chiming in with recollections of decoying ducks or whiffling geese that seemed plated with Kevlar! Dropping shots may look easy, but they seldom are!

The reason most hunters find falling targets so difficult to hit is because this shot has not been a part of traditional shotgunner

An experienced coach is an invaluable tool in improving shooting skills on the range or in the field.

training. Those who came to wingshooting through trap, skeet or even informal hand-thrown targets have seldom had to deal with a dropping target in a "practice" setting where they could concentrate on learning how to hit it.

Quite to the contrary, shooters learning trap and skeet are always encouraged to break the target at or before the apex of the flight path because it's "easier to do." That is the infancy of a self-predatory cycle. Obviously it's easier to hit the target on the way up if that's all you ever practice.

Yet the dropping shot is one that every extreme waterfowl hunter is faced with almost every time he or she steps in the blind. And even we have been encouraged over the years to pick rising, going-away shots rather than incoming, dropping shots. It is a belief still held by some old-time waterfowlers that shot penetrated better on ducks and geese going away because the pellets would slip between the feathers more easily than punching through them "against the grain" on an incoming shot. The extreme waterfowler's goal should be to bring the birds into ranges where that isn't going to matter much to begin with. Our shots should be centered on the vulnerable, lightly-feathered head and neck, anyway.

Except, perhaps, for a few waterfowl guides who hunt every day of the season in several states, there are no hunters today who

A good day doesn't have to mean lots of shooting, but this crew has a lot to smile about.

get enough shooting opportunities each season to perfect the falling target shot strictly on real birds. The advent of sporting clays is what has made the average wingshooter more conscious of his lacking ability to hit rapidly ground-bound targets. Sporting clays courses are set up in such a way that on many waterfowl simulating stations, the target is not visible or not in range until it is descending and decelerating much like a duck dropping into the decoys. There's no option to rise up and flare the bird and hold off until it's rising and going away. You either hit the target as it drops or score a loss.

It only takes scorecards from a couple of rounds to reveal weaknesses in shooting abilities. Because of the traditional training background of most wingshooters, the falling target weakness is one that frequently shows up.

Another way to find out whether the falling target is your weakness is to go out to the springing teal station on your favorite course. Shoot ten targets on which you make a conscious effort to break the target on the way up or at the peak of its flight. Then shoot ten targets on which you wait to mount the gun until the bird is falling back to the ground. Most shooters will score significantly higher on the first ten targets.

Hitting dropping targets on the course or in the blind is not impossible. In fact, it can become easy if you set about practicing it with purpose. Exhibition shooters can consistently hand lob half a dozen or more targets in the air and break each one with an individual shot before they hit the ground. Obviously, the majority of these targets are broken as they fall, the final ones just a short distance from the ground. It can be done *with practice.*

The key, just as in hitting crossing and outgoing targets, is a smooth, consistent swing and follow-through. You keep the barrel moving, you might hit the target. You stop the barrel, and you're sure to miss.

Because we've practiced so much on rising and outgoing targets, our bodies and eyes have learned what it takes to hit them. Swinging the gun up and through these targets feels natural. Based on experience, you can usually tell whether such a shot is going to be on the mark even before you see the target break or the bird fold. It becomes "instinctive" shooting.

On the other hand, the unfamiliar motion of tracking a descending target feels unnatural. That unnatural feel and mental lack of confidence in the shot are what cause the brain to backfire and coerce you into stopping your swing even though you *know* you must follow through to hit the target.

At first, as you get the hang of it, you'll probably find yourself breaking targets you thought were going to be misses because the shot still doesn't feel right. By practicing the dropping shot with purpose, the "feel" will come.

One trick recommended by shooting coaches in learning any shot is to exaggerate the motion. On a range where it can be done safely, maintain the swing well after the gun is fired. Try to continue moving even as the gun is taken from shoulder and the action opened. By exaggerating the motion, you will likely find that you concentrate better on making arms, body, head and gun swing as one unit no matter which direction a target is tracked.

Practice with a purpose will turn mechanical skills into instinct. When your wingshooting becomes instinctive, when your shotgun feels as natural as your own limbs, you will know you've taken another step closer to being an extreme waterfowl hunter.

Resources To Improve Your Waterfowling Wingshooting

Here are some places to begin your search for improvement of your waterfowl wingshooting skills:

Shoot Where You Look
Leon Measures
Dept. NAH
408 Fair Street
Livingston, TX 77351
Or you can call Leon at (713) 457-1250 or (409) 327-5358.

Federal Wing & Clay School
Dept. NAH
15 Furman Crescent
Rochester, NY 14620
(800) 888-WING (9464)

Remington Shooting School
Dept. NAH
14 Hoefler Avenue
Ilion, NY 13357
(800) 742-7053

5

Extreme Dogs
For Extreme Hunters

The reason extreme waterfowl hunters *hunt* over well-trained retrievers is because they know that there is no greater conservation measure than a good dog. It doesn't take many days in the company of even a mediocre retriever to appreciate that a dog will find downed birds that no human hunter could ever recover. Even the most extreme waterfowl hunter has nothing in the repertoire that can compare to a dog's sense of smell and instinct for the hunt.

The reason extreme waterfowl hunters *own* retrievers is because dogs are the ultimate year-round link to hunting. The care and training required to maximize the great potential of a well-bred retriever is a seven days a week, 365 days a year commitment that lasts for anywhere from 10 to 15 years! Not everyone is willing to make that commitment, but the extreme waterfowl hunter will find a way. The rewards are many and frequent.

There's a warm glow in the hunter's soul with every little triumph in training, with each great retrieve, on good days and bad days shared with an unquestioning companion, even from the smell of wet dog lingering in the truck. Yet the greatest reward of dog ownership for the extreme waterfowl hunter is the privilege of sharing life with a creature who lives for the hunt even more than we do! Every time you scratch those ears, every time you look into those eyes, though it might be the middle of June, you go hunting together.

The extreme waterfowl hunter *hunts* over good retrievers. The complete extreme waterfowler's soul is *owned* by at least one.

The Making Of Extreme Retrievers

The training of a dog to become an extreme retriever is beyond the scope of this book. Hundreds of books and videos exist to teach you how to do that. Hundreds of professional dog trainers put food on the table for their families by molding extreme waterfowl hunters and extreme retrievers into efficient teams. Becoming a really good dog trainer, professional or amateur, is a lifetime pursuit. Good teachers are always learning themselves!

Instead, we'll look at how to find and mold a pup in those first, crucial months to give it the best possible shot at becoming an extreme retriever. We'll look at setting goals for your dog and make some recommendations on how to achieve them.

Two dogs? Twice the fun! The extreme waterfowler will always have a young dog on the way up to take the place of a veteran who has served its master well!

Finding The Right Puppy

If there were one perfect name for every retriever pup ever whelped, it must be "Potential." At least that's the way it feels when you peer into a whelping box to watch that mass of newborn, canine enthusiasm squirm and wrestle for the best nursing spots. You can't help but believe that there's an extreme retriever in the bunch. Yet at the same time, you're likely to feel overwhelmed at the prospect of figuring out which it is.

Across the spectrum of the retriever breeds, there is a right dog for every extreme waterfowl hunter willing to make the commitment of time, energy and money to create an extreme retrieving companion. The hard part is matching up the right owner with the right pup from the thousands of litters of Labradors, Chesapeakes, Goldens, Flatcoats, Springers and others whelped every year.

Obviously the first decision in selecting the right puppy for you and your family is choosing the breed you want. Selecting the breed of your extreme retriever has to be a personal choice primarily based on your own experience with various breeds and the research you put in at the library and by talking to trainers and breeders. If you've hunted over a particular breed of retriever and liked what you saw, contact that dog's owner. Be prepared with a list of questions, not so much about that breed's traits in the field because you've seen what that dog can do. Instead, ask the owner how difficult it was to train the dog to reach that level of performance. Ask what everyday life is like with that breed during the "off-season." Ask about special health concerns or requirements that might be unique to the breed. Ask how the dog would fit into the lifestyle around your home.

Since we're talking about finding an "extreme retriever" for the extreme waterfowl hunter, we'll stick with the breeds developed primarily for retrieving web-footed fowl under any conditions from baking sun in dusty fields to freezing rain and frigid waves. *Speaking in general terms* that means we'll stick to the Labrador, the Chesapeake, the Golden and the water spaniels. Now if you have a springer or a short-tailed pointer or even a poodle who does extreme work and thrives in the extreme conditions, please don't close this book offended. Just realize that the odds of plucking a future extreme retriever from a whelping box of your breed are lower than from a box of Labs, Goldens or Chessies. The goal here is to give the extreme waterfowl hunter the best of chance of choosing a dog that will match his hunting style.

Since it is the most popular breed of dog in America (as shown by American Kennel Club registrations), let's assume for our example that you've decided a Labrador is best going to suit your hunting needs, your abilities as a trainer and your family's lifestyle. The same procedures and advice will hold true no matter what breed you've actually decided on.

The most important step is narrowing your choice down to *the* right litter. The research you put into finding *the* litter will have the greatest influence on your chances of selecting the best pup for you.

At this early stage in the process, you need to determine about how much you're willing to spend on a pup. If you turn to the classified ads in a good-sized city's Sunday newspaper, you'll likely find a dozen or more ads for litters of Lab puppies.

Most of these newspaper ads are likely to be for litters from backyard breeders. Prices for these pups with all their shots will likely run anywhere from $250 to $600, depending on the part of the country where you're looking. You'll also note that most of these ads are for litters on the ground or due in the near future. If this is the price range where you are looking, there's nothing wrong with buying a pup from a backyard breeder if you're willing to go in with your eyes open and ask lots of questions.

In this scenario, the most important question is "why did you have this litter of pups?" If the breeder's response is something like, "because we wanted the kids to experience the miracle of birth" or "my female's a good water dog and my buddy's got a great pheasant hunting male, so we figured..." thank them for their time and cross them off the list of prospects.

However, if the answer is "well my female is from the XYZ line with so-and-so and so-and-so in her pedigree, and we found that a number of examples of successful crosses of this line with the ABC line..." you've got a good prospect. Though the people you're dealing with may not be "professional" breeders, they have taken a professional attitude toward what they are doing.

The other option for finding a litter from which to select your pup is to look at the ads in sporting dog publications. The ads you'll find here are most likely from professional breeders and/or dedicated amateurs with the professional attitude. Depending on the accomplishments of the male and female and the "lines" from which the pups will be produced, prices will range from $500 up. Pups from parents who have proven themselves in competition and hunt tests will probably go for well over $1,000 apiece.

Remember, bringing home a puppy is a 10 to 15 year commitment to the training, health and comfort of a retriever.

In either case, your basic research tools are going to be pedigrees or "family trees" of the litter in which you are interested. Get a pedigree for the litter from the breeder. If they won't supply one, find one who will.

A pedigree is going to show you the accomplishments of your pup's ancestors. In the case of a retriever to be used primarily for hunting, you'll want to see a good number of ancestors with field trial and hunting test titles. The letters to look for are FC, AFC, CFC, CAFC, JH, SH, MH, HR, MHR, GMHR among others.

Now just because a dog doesn't have a title before or after its name doesn't mean it wasn't somebody's great hunting dog, but without personal experience with that dog, you have no way of knowing. At least the titles show that the dog was trainable, was able to mark and had the drive and intelligence to make it in some highly competitive hunting-like contests.

While a lot of titled dogs in a pedigree is great, the pup is naturally going to inherit most of its abilities and potential directly from its parents. Those are the two dogs you should give the closest scrutiny to in selecting the litter. If at all possible, make arrangements to see both of these dogs actually hunting or at least in a serious training session. If you become familiar with the sire and the dam, you'll be amazed how much of them you'll see in your pup as it progresses through its training!

You'll likely find two or three litters that seem to meet all your criteria and have nearly equally distinguished pedigrees. A big part of the final decision on which litter to choose can sometimes be based on what type of guarantee the breeder is willing to give you.

At minimum you should expect, in writing, a guarantee for the purchase price on the soundness of the pup's hips, elbows and eyes, and any other genetic defects which may surface in the first two to three years of the pup's life. The guarantee should include delivery of the pup in a healthy condition along with a certified record of vaccinations. You should also be given the name and phone number of the vet who handled the prenatal care of the bitch and the care of the litter including vaccinations, check-ups, dew claw removal, tail docking and any other appropriate procedures.

You've selected the litter and you've got money down on a pup. You're happy with the blank sales contract and guarantee you have in your hands. The day has come to pick your puppy; to take home a companion for the next 10, 12 or 15 years.

Before you head for the kennel, there's one more big decision to make—do you take your family along to be part of the decision? If you're truly serious about finding the right puppy for your family, the answer may surprise you. Leave them at home!

The person who will be the primary care-giver and trainer of the dog should go to pick the pup by himself or

The result of selecting the right pup and seeing to it the dog achieves its full potential is a well-oiled team!

There are days of great fun ahead for the pup in the arms of this extreme waterfowl hunter!

herself. Alone, you'll have the best odds of making a good decision based on sound judgment and practical analysis rather than which pup licked who the most and which one has "the prettiest eyes."

Once you've made your choice, gather the pup up in your arms, take it home and play the hero by bursting through the door announcing, "Here's our new puppy!" If you employ the family's help in naming the wriggling new addition, there will be no hurt feelings.

All that leaves is picking a puppy from the litter, and as you can tell from the space devoted to it here, there isn't a great deal of scientific advice to give. Sometimes you can do just as well by wearing a blindfold and reaching into the whelping box. Remember, in a well-chosen litter, every one of the pups likely could be named "Potential."

As much chance as there is to it, there are a few things you can do in selecting a pup from a litter that help put your mind at ease if nothing else. They are designed to determine the pup's drive, bird desire and nose.

The first test is to roll the pup over on its back and pin it there lightly with your hand on its belly and around its front legs. If the pup struggles hard and continuously, it's likely to be on the hard-driving and aggressive end of the scale. If it immediately submits and doesn't struggle, it's likely to be a submissive dog without much drive. A dog that struggles, then submits, struggles and submits is somewhere in the middle. Depending on the extreme waterfowl hunter's training experience or willingness to use a professional trainer and what he or she is expecting of the dog at home, the pup that struggles and submits, struggles and submits or the constant struggler would likely be the right choice.

By the way, each of these tests should be conducted with the pup that's under consideration away from the rest of the litter. Pups will frequently behave much differently when they are away from the comfortable litter surroundings, and on their own is likely how they'll serve out the majority of their hunting careers.

The second test is to present the pup with a wing-clipped pigeon. Simply judge the reaction of the pups under consideration against one another. For an extreme retriever, birdiness is of utmost importance. Proper socialization will enhance bird desire, but the more it is innate, the easier building that excitement will be. If this is the first time the pup has been around birds, so much the better because then this test will also reveal more of the personality characteristics described in the first test.

The downfall of this test is that any pup can have an off day when it is more interested in chewing on your socks or sleeping than in birds. It's best if you can visit the pups two or three times to give them an opportunity to prove themselves. Ask the breeder to mark your best prospects with a certain color collar or a permanent marker dot inside the ear. It's amazing how mixed up even the breeder can get as the puppies change from day to day.

The last test is to put out a fresh-killed pigeon or even a small dish of dog food in a clump of grass or a bush. Take the prospect out, play

with it and casually walk downwind of the seductive smell. If the pup pounces, then at least you know its nose works.

Based primarily on careful research and soul-searching about what you want your new dog to ultimately accomplish, and based a little bit on some head-to-head testing, you can be confident your next pup will be worthy of the name "Potential."

Contributing To The Success Of Your Extreme Retriever

The first step is selecting the right litter and the right puppy. The second step is the most important in ensuring that any dog is given the best chance to achieve its full potential, and it's one of which you are in complete control. It's the period of a puppy's life called socialization. That's a fancy way of saying teaching your young dog how to learn!

While hunting an area where several blinds and decoy spreads are situated on the same marsh, we've all watched a flock of ducks work another hunter's blocks, then commit. Suddenly a bird cartwheels and falls while

You contribute to your dog's success by making it as easy and comfortable as possible for it to do the job. That's what floatation vests do!

the rest of the flock flares and wings away. A moment later the sound of the shot reaches your ears.

For someone uninitiated in hunting, this order of events might seem unnatural, but for those who know what it takes to lure in a flock of birds and make eyes and hands work in tandem for a killing shot, the lag in hearing the shot is understood.

The case is the same in watching a great performance by an extreme retriever. A novice seeing such a performance for the first time would assume this is the way all dogs work. It takes a veteran to realize all the work and training nuances that went into creating a great retriever—and the order in which they happened.

Socialization is the mortar that will hold together all the other training building blocks. And like the distant shot in the marsh, the results of proper socialization, as important as they are, may not be recognized for months or years into a dog's career.

A picture perfect retrieve is as much the result of proper socialization as it is of training or bloodlines.

The importance of proper socialization in achieving top, lifelong performance from any dog cannot be over stressed. Pro trainers see it all the time. Two pups will come into the kennel both at about five or six months of age. One carries a pedigree that reads like a "Who's Who" of the field trial world. The second has a few FCs and MHs in the lineage, but they're scattered and back a couple generations or more.

The hotshot pup was purchased by a well-to-do owner who wants a great dog to show off to his buddies, but either because of lack of knowledge or because of the time he spends making the kind of money he used to pay for the pup, the youngster has barely been out of the kennel for a half hour a day, if that.

The run-of-the-mill pup belongs to a family whose main intent was to have it as a pet for the kids and have it hunt a few times a year if things worked out. But during the time they've owned it, the pup has taken two family vacations, goes to town several times a week, romps in the park every day, chases the local golf course goose population and simply has seen a lot of life.

All else being equal, like the kids not having instilled a ton of bad habits in young "Run Of The Mill," the less pedigreed puppy will be easier to train with faster and more lasting results. Proper socialization will allow any trainer to overcome a world of other shortcomings because a well-socialized dog knows *how to learn*.

One of the greatest losses to the retriever world is a puppy of great bloodlines with all that potential going for it virtually ruined by lack of socialization. Such a pup is never given a chance to succeed. The goal of socialization is to produce a dog that is confident and self-assured, yet attentive and cognitive of the owner/trainer as the source of assistance when it's necessary. The process of socialization is giving the pup as many "life experiences" as possible at a young age, while making sure that the pup stays safe and healthy while gaining them.

To achieve the socialization goal it's best to approach it with a game plan. However, remember that each dog is an individual, so time lines will vary. Determining when a dog is ready for a particular socialization step is part of your education in reading your dog.

The most important period for thorough and diverse

Remember that everything you do with your dog is a team effort with you as the captain.

socialization is from the time you pick up the pup at seven or eight weeks through its sixth month. This is when a pup really learns how to learn—with you as teacher.

Specifically, during this time in a retriever's life it must have daily, extended human contact with an emphasis on learning simple right-from-wrong concepts. It's essential that the owner, trainer or whoever is spending time with the pup be firm but fair in helping the pup learn what is acceptable behavior and what is not. Consistency and routine are key to instilling this understanding.

Expanding the pup's environmental experiences are also critical. Work on water confidence in controlled situations where you can be certain that nothing it will perceive as "bad" will happen to the dog while it's in the water. Along with this goes positive introductions to the myriad of equipment that will become an important part of the dog's life. Decoys, boats, leads, slip collars, dummy collars, duck blinds, goose calls, waders and hippers, platforms, crates, oars and a hundred other pieces of gear need to be presented in a non-threatening manner. The pup must come to recognize that these mean it's time to go to work, but to a job the dog loves more than life itself.

Same goes for introducing the pup to new types of cover. During this time it should feel everything from swamp muck, to wheat stubble, to alfalfa, to plowed ground, to rocks, to snow under its pads. It should be exposed to a diversity of kennels, vehicles, houses and buildings. The life of an extreme retriever is a life of travel and daily changes in weather, surroundings and routine. Diverse experiences as a pup lay a strong mental foundation for a dog who can take life as it comes and stay focused on the job.

Initial exposure to live birds should come early in the socialization period with the goal of enhancing innate desire. Again, this is done by introducing the pup to live birds in situations where you can positively prevent anything "bad" from happening to the pup. In other words, *don't introduce the pop of a shotgun during those initial encounters with birds!*

The goal here is to make the young retriever love everything about birds. The young dog must come to live for birds and believe that nothing bad will ever happen to him when birds are involved. If that means a youngster eats a pigeon or two early on, then so be it.

The gun should only be introduced after total confidence with birds is deeply ingrained. Association of the gun with birds should be done slowly! A muffled cap pistol at first, then light blanks at a distance, then heavy blanks and finally a shotgun. And the gun should only be fired when the dog is totally focused on birds. The gun becomes a signal that the dog will get to interact with birds—the thing it now lives for above all else.

With desire and life experiences established as the pup reaches or passes six months of age, it's now okay to start using more discipline and some pressure to reduce bad habits. This is done in two ways. First, obviously, by becoming more demanding on known commands when it is called for. Secondly, and more importantly, by redoubling the effort of praising pup when it does things right.

Positive reinforcement is the basis of all socialization, but it's supported with avoidance or negative reinforcement. A big part of learning to learn is gaining the ability to learn from mistakes. In the later socialization process and through all the rest of a retriever's lifelong training there will be times when you set the dog up to succeed and there will be times you set it up to fail. Success allows for positive reinforcement and the building of confidence. Failure allows for correction which is also an important teacher of the properly socialized dog. It is important, though, that the socialization come first so that the dog is mentally prepared to handle failure, understand correction and learn from it.

What Will You Expect Of Your Extreme Retriever?

Different waterfowl hunters are going to have different expectations of their dogs. Some will be happy if a dog sits still enough not to spook incoming birds, exits the blind on its own accord and goes most of the way to a downed bird on the water by running the shoreline. As long as "Rover" brings the birds back to the blind before he drops them, that hunter is content.

It's likely the extreme waterfowl hunter is going to expect much more. He or she wants a retriever who keeps a constant watch for birds, who sits rock steady until given the command to move. He or she will expect the dog to take a straight line to every bird it sees fall, regardless of what lays in the path, and to return by that same line. Such a dog must remember or "mark" at least two or three birds down with confidence. For those birds the dog doesn't see fall, it has to handle quickly and crisply—knowing when to rely on "master" and when to take charge. This dog must accept that dead birds are to be picked up only after wounded and hidden birds are recovered.

Maybe the best way to look at it is by comparing what you expect out of your hunting dog in the field to what you might demand from your vehicle on the road.

Many drivers go happily through life with a utilitarian vehicle like a mini-van. Today's standard of the suburbs sure isn't much to look at, no one ever labels them "responsive handlers," seldom are they built to surround you in luxury. But they reliably get the driver from point A to point B and offer the utility of doing it while carrying a big load.

Then there are those drivers who simply must have "the best" complete with the luxury package; "loaded" is the term we often hear. It's these folks who keep Cadillac and Lincoln and Mercedes and BMW in business.

The ultimate goal of both groups of drivers is to get from point A to point B. Both groups of vehicles can get the job done. The difference is just a matter of what two different drivers expect from the ride.

So it is with hunters. Though ultimately the goal for every hunting retriever is to find and bring back birds, each dog owner must come to grips with how efficiently, how professionally, how comfortably and how beautifully the job must be done.

The true extreme waterfowl hunter, without question, wants to name his dog Mercedes or Caddy! But there's only one way the extreme waterfowl hunter can justly set that level of performance goals from a retriever. He or she must make a commitment to training for the life of the dog. Only a small portion of such performance is "instinctive" for any retriever; the rest must be learned from a fair and consistent teacher.

There needs to be a good bit of soul searching that goes into the decision to own a dog of such potential. Do you have the experience and knowledge to train the dog yourself? Are you willing to commit the financial resources to have the dog professionally trained? Even if you go with a professional trainer, recognize that there will still be a big time commitment on your part to learn to "read" the dog and in learning how to play your vital part in the team.

If you're willing to make the commitment, then the rewards of owning and hunting over an extreme retriever are among the greatest to be found in hunting or any of the other less-extreme sports.

6

Extreme Scouting

Though it takes on different characteristics depending on what part of North America you do your waterfowl hunting in, scouting is a vital part of the successful hunting equation for every extreme waterfowl hunter. There are actually three types or three tiers of scouting for waterfowl. The first is preseason scouting. Then there is daily scouting during the season. And finally there is micro-scouting of the precise area you intend to hunt. All three must be mastered in the extreme waterfowler's repertoire.

Preseason Scouting

Scouting before the season for waterfowl is different than preseason scouting for any type of non-migratory bird or animal. You don't have the advantage of seeing the game or utilizing those sightings to understand the animal's daily pattern.

Preseason scouting for ducks and geese is largely keeping tabs of what's going on in your hunting area. What is the status of wetlands and water levels? If you hunt lakes, has there been new development on the shoreline? In the marsh, have there been any projects that will change open areas? If field hunting is on the menu, what's been planted where and how is the harvest predicted to go?

Good preseason scouting relies largely on either an excellent memory or well-kept records. To predict what the birds are likely to do when they return to the area, you must know what they did previously when conditions were similar. For example, the last time the summer was dry, your best hunting area may have been on a particular bend on the main channel of a permanent river or on a rocky point jutting out into a large lake with little vegetation. Yet in a wet year when there are potholes and sloughs scattered throughout the countryside and rivers are surrounded by shallow back waters, there will be no sense in hitting the dry year reliables.

Building a file of hunting and scouting journals and well-used maps is one of the best ways to prevent confusion about what each season was like. By comparing the conditions recorded in those logs, you'll be able to make more accurate predictions about what the birds will do when conditions are similar. And even then, those fickle birds usually find a way to fool us!

The best scouts are those extreme waterfowl hunters lucky enough to live right in their hunting areas for many years. One such extreme waterfowl hunter is Dawn Charging of Bismarck, North Dakota. Dawn was born and raised among the prairie potholes of that hunters' paradise and was taught the ways of the ducks and geese that pour through the state each autumn by her mom, Tolly Holtan. Tolly tells stories of taking Dawn hunting when she was small enough to wrap in a blanket and hide under a shell decoy!

Dawn has spent more than 25 seasons in the fields and sloughs of the region surrounding Lake Sakakawea. In fact, she and Tolly have both been licensed waterfowl guides there at one time or another. For them, preseason scouting is less of a conscious effort than a natural observation of what's going on in the area. Because they've lived and ranched and farmed there all their lives, they have developed a highly intuitive second nature about what the birds will likely do during various parts of the season. You name any date in October and November, and Dawn can name half a dozen places scattered over several hundred square miles or more where you're likely to have a good hunt if the birds are in.

While all extreme waterfowl hunters strive to live the waterfowling lifestyle year round, few of us are lucky enough to live in the midst of our hunting grounds year-round! We have to take our chances with maps, notes and legwork to improve our chances when the birds come back!

Tolly Holtan is one of those lucky extreme waterfowlers who lives in her hunting area. Scouting is part of the routine of daily life for her.

Preseason Scouting Taken To The Extreme

Given the chance, extreme waterfowl hunters will take their preseason scouting, like everything else, to the extreme. The results can be outstanding for the hunter willing to expend some effort, imagination and, perhaps, some money.

Say for example you do a great deal of your hunting on a particular large public marsh. Most of it is cattails interspersed with open water areas. Some of these are connected by navigable channels and some are isolated.

Sitting in your boat at water level, it probably looks like you're on the only open water in the marsh. Maps published by the U.S. Geologic Survey, state or county, help broaden the picture, but only show the channels and the larger bodies of water, and they are not updated very often. Floods, drought and the work of beavers can change the lay of the semi-land drastically from season to season.

As you glide down the channels in your boat checking out spots that have been good in seasons past, you can't help but recall watching flocks of those big late season mallards landing a quarter mile behind where you were set up. The little patch of trees on the horizon back there seemed to swallow them up.

The hunter who floated his canoe up on this spot has struck gold!

What's back there, anyway? You know there's no way in by boat because you've tried to get there half a dozen different ways. And where exactly was the spot? Though you might make it back there in your waders to check it out, it doesn't seem likely you'd actually find it by pushing blindly through the thick, tall cover.

When faced with such a situation, the extreme waterfowl hunter takes to the air! In an airplane ride of just an hour or two you could likely map and record GPS coordinates for every acre or bigger spot of open water on the marsh. Splitting the cost of the flight with a hunting buddy or two who would love to have that information makes aerial scouting mighty practical.

Armed with that information you could map out the shortest "over slough" route to drag, pull, push or carry a small canoe or coffin blind, and you could be waiting for those mallards next time they come in!

Aerial scouting also works great in large areas of flooded timber to pinpoint openings the ducks will flock to. And

Aerial scouting is undoubtedly extreme but very effective. Take video or still shots from the area to review at home.

there's no faster way to get an overall picture of what's planted where and how the growing season is going than by chartering a flight over your favorite field hunting areas. Plus you're getting the added benefit of seeing the terrain much as your quarry sees it!

Daily Scouting During The Season

This is the kind of scouting most every waterfowl hunter is familiar with, especially goose hunters who follow the birds from midday loafing areas to feeding fields in the late afternoon. With luck, the birds will be going back to the same field the next morning, and hopefully, with the landowner's permission, you'll be set up to greet them when they do.

Daily scouting isn't much more than that. You drive around in known waterfowl haunts during the midday hours trying to spot birds. A prime location to get started is a hill looking over a waterfowl resting area. When birds start to head out to feed, try to determine the flight path the birds seem to be taking. Maneuver underneath that path, then pick a promising looking flock and try to follow them.

This type of scouting is best accomplished with at least two people in the vehicle! The driver can concentrate on driving and finding roads leading in the same direction the birds are going. The passenger can concentrate on the traveling flock, call out course changes to the driver and keep an eye on the map for shortcuts the driver might not know about.

While this may seem like simply racing the birds to a feeding area, smart scouts also keep an eye out for likely spots to intercept birds between the feeding area and the main midday roost. This is particularly effective if you're hunting ducks, which can be more fickle than geese about where they feed. Geese will usually return morning and night to the same feeding area until they clean out the field or until hunting pressure drives them out of the area. Ducks, on the other hand, seem to change feeding areas at the drop of a hat, often for no reason human hunters can recognize.

However, ducks can often be intercepted at sloughs and potholes between the feeding field and the large midday resting area. If conditions in the feeding area are dry, they'll often head immediately to the nearest hole for water to aid in digestion of their meal. And maybe they are just being lazy, looking for a safe resting place closer to the feed. Whatever the reason, smart scouts will be on the lookout for ambush places to intercept the birds when they are done feeding. The beauty of locating such a honey hole is that you can sleep in, set up on the slough while the ducks are in the field and have great "banker's hours" shooting! Though for the extreme waterfowl hunter it's mighty tough to let a sunrise slip by; each one is a new experience to add to the collection.

Another great place to begin daily scouting is at the post office, in a local watering hole, at the gas station, at the feed mill or any other small town gathering place in waterfowl country. Landowners and townsfolk like the school bus driver, mail delivery people, the propane or fuel oil delivery driver or the waiter in the local cafe can all be valuable resources on where to begin that day's scouting mission.

Particularly in snow goose country, it's not uncommon for farmers to come into town looking for hunters to come shoot birds on their places! Light geese come in such great numbers they can devastate crops. And in the spring, when those birds are headed north, they can really put a hurt on the wallet of the farmer whose land is "blessed" by their visit. Farmers realize that the fewer birds come back, the less damage they'll do!

Tools For Extreme Scouting

For daily scouting missions, you can get by with a 4x4 vehicle, a good partner and a better memory. However, a few "high tech" tools will make your scouting missions more efficient and more successful.

Good binoculars makes watching the birds more interesting and more educational. By being eight or ten times closer through the glasses, you can tell what the birds are doing and how they are interacting in the flock, which can be valuable knowledge when you're setting a decoy spread. Additionally, binoculars make it easier to spot birds against a dark horizon. They make it easier to pinpoint precisely where in a field or marsh the birds are landing.

Especially in a situation where hunters are "competing" to find the best fields to hunt in, a cellular phone puts you ahead in the game. If you arrive at a field the geese are using, you can check out the name and possibly phone number listed on any "no hunting" signs and contact the landowner while you're standing at the edge of the field watching the birds land. The most current plat book available is a great tool to use in combination with the cell phone in cases where you aren't sure who owns the piece of land the birds are ravaging.

Though the cellular phone can put you in touch with a landowner more quickly than the hunter who has to go racing off to find him, it's still good to try to meet the landowner once you've secured permission. A handshake, a personal greeting from someone who is well-kept and well-spoken, a promise to respect the property and perhaps a gift or token payment or the offer of some help around the

A brace of birds can be a welcome gift to the landowner who's given you permission to hunt on his property. Always clean the birds before offering them to him.

place, all go a long way in improving the overall image of hunters. That and perhaps a visit or two during preseason scouting can sew up first crack at a good hunting spot for seasons to come, too!

One big hint in landowner relations. If the farmer and his family indicate they would be interested in some birds for their table you should certainly oblige, but don't look on them as a way to get rid of undressed birds. Farm life, particularly during the harvest season, is hectic enough. No farmer who has just put in 14 or 18 hours in the combine or corn picker is going to relish the thought of drawing and picking a dozen geese before he goes to bed! That sort of thing will sour him on hunters and their "tokens of appreciation."

If the farmer does want some birds, dress them yourself or have them picked by a cleaning service. Inspect them carefully and give the farmer birds that are the least shot up and look most like you'd be buying out of the freezer at the grocery store. Wrap them up in fresh, clear plastic bags or freezer wrap. Have them frozen solid if possible, or at least well-cooled. Consider throwing a nice cooler into the bargain and place the birds into it on plenty of ice. It might be some time before the farmer or the family will be able to get them into the freezer or perhaps a meat locker in town.

The highest of the high-tech scouting gear is a handheld Global Positioning System. These incredible units will give you your precise location 24 hours a day. Best of all, they will record it and guide you back to that location easily, even in the predawn darkness the next morning.

The Global Positioning System works by simple triangulation. When the unit is turned on, it locks on to at least three satellites, usually more, of the dozens orbiting the earth. The receiver then "finds" itself in relationship to those satellites and reads out the location and even the elevation. You then command it to mark the spot as a retrievable waypoint, which you give a name. When you call up that name later on, the unit will tell you which direction and how far you are from that waypoint.

Some units also offer plotting capabilities, which are especially nice for the extreme waterfowl hunter who has located a spot to hunt in the morning just as darkness settles in. Using the plotting function, you can take the shortest way back to camp marking each change of direction on the GPS unit. In the morning, you simple recall that miniature "map" and you can retrace your steps back to the exact spot you want to hunt even if you've only been there once before in the dark! A handheld GPS can easily put you within just a few yards of the spot you marked as your waypoint!

GPS units offer a wide range of capabilities depending on price. Some of the newest models from Eagle feature map chips that you plug into the back of the unit. You simply call up the map for the area you are hunting, place the pointer on spots you want to check out and start zooming in. You'll see roads, lakes, rivers, towns, etc. just like you would on a regular map! Handheld GPS units run from about $100 up to $1,000 depending on capabilities. Of course you still need to carry a compass because it has no batteries that could give out, but a GPS can guide you to some great duck and goose hunting sites you might never have been able to find, or at least find again, without one!

Micro-Scouting

Not every waterfowl hunter has to preseason scout or will have the opportunity to preseason scout. If you live far from your hunting grounds, it might not be possible to convince the family to use part of its summer vacation time to go map cornfields and potholes. If you live in your hunting grounds, preseason scouting is more precisely just keeping your eyes open to what's going on through the summer.

Many waterfowl hunters don't even have to do daily scouting. If you have a particular blind or even acreage leased for the season, there's not a lot of point driving around watching birds going into other peoples' leases.

Micro-scouting is a system of scouting that can benefit every single extreme waterfowl hunter, yet it's probably done less than the others combined. Even under its more common name, "bird watching," most waterfowl hunters do far too little of it.

Dawn Charging has refined micro-scouting to a science! She's the one who gave me a great appreciation of what it can do to boost hunting success when you're actually in the field.

If it has webbed feet, Dawn is fanatical about hunting it, but she specializes in taking Canada geese—greaters and giants in particular. When Dawn has pinpointed a field she plans to hunt, she'll watch the birds work it. She'll glass the birds coming into the field and on the ground for hours, sometimes over the course of several days before hunting the field.

When she goes into the field to set a decoy spread, she knows what parts of the field the birds like best and what parts they avoid. She'll know where the greaters and giants are feeding in relationship to the lessers and perhaps snows and whitefronts that might be there.

She'll know the approximate size of the family groups of the big geese. Of perhaps 500 or 1,000 birds that are using a particular field, only 100 or a couple of dozen are ten-pounders, and

Dawn Charging is a master of micro-scouting. She often watches a field of birds for several days before she hunts it!

Dawn will know how many. She'll know if there are any other hunter's spreads within a mile or so of "her field." She'll know if there are any buildings or trees in the immediate area from which the birds are shying. She'll know which direction the birds are tending to feed in different winds. And she'll have decided precisely where the decoys should be set, in what numbers and where the gunners should hide.

That's a lot more than just bird watching. That's micro-scouting done by an extreme goose hunter!

Doing more micro-scouting could help waterfowl hunters everywhere. Take for example an individual levy blind leased by a couple of duck hunters in a California, Arkansas or Louisiana rice field. Though leased by the season, most of these blinds are let under an agreement that they'll only be hunted two or three days per week. Use those off days to take a lawn chair, some binoculars and some cold beverages and watch your field from a nearby road or unhunted field.

Pay special attention to what time the birds come to the field and from which direction. Note which species of ducks are the first to arrive and what the species ratio is of birds working the field. Are the birds coming in big flocks to boost numbers quickly or are they straggling in to create a slowly growing flock? See what else is around the blind besides ducks. Are there shorebirds which normally spook at your first shots? How about herons, egrets or coot? Watch carefully and make yourself some drawings of what parts of the field the birds prefer to use, and how closely together they sit on the water. Use different symbols for different species to determine which ducks are going where on the field.

Even with the spaced out days of hunting, birds in these areas can be highly pressured. By late in the season they've been hunted for as long as five months straight. They have every reason to fear any set-up that doesn't look completely natural. The attention the extreme waterfowl hunter devotes to these small details while micro-scouting can make the difference in setting a spread that will lure even the wariest birds within range.

It's almost a prerequisite that you be an unabashed bird watcher to earn the title of extreme waterfowl hunter. It's a title we should wear proudly because it's only by watching the birds that we can learn how to get closer to them. John Audubon, a fine wingshot and certainly an early-day extreme waterfowl hunter, would be proud!

7

Extreme Attention
To Detail

*T*hough wind-burned, cracked and bleeding fingers may be evidence of a different tale, the extreme waterfowl hunter loves to set decoys. Whether the scene is a dusty field of wheat stubble, a tiny opening in a shallowly flooded oak bottom, the manmade pond in front of an assigned state blind or whitecaps cresting at two feet beyond sight of shore, every setup is a new, fresh challenge. Even if you've set the same spread a thousand times before, every block is placed carefully in "just the right spot" to maximize the illusion.

It's in the selection of the decoys themselves and the price paid for them. It's in the rigging and the maintenance. It's in the selection of the hunting spot. It's in the effort expended to transport the decoys where they must go to be effective. It's in the care and thought with which the spread is set. It's in the willingness to pack 'em up and take 'em home. This is where the extreme waterfowl hunter reveals his or her true dedication. Remember, to the extreme waterfowl hunter, no effort is too great in the pursuit of birds and memories.

Ducks and geese can be killed over a string of a dozen empty bleach bottles painted half black or a field full of plastic garbage bags on a day when the mood strikes the birds to come in. They can also be pass-shot or jump-shot, and there's nothing wrong with those methods if that's the experience you wish to collect that day.

But to the true extreme waterfowl hunter, bringing the birds close—truly, 100 percent, completely fooling them—is the name of the game. Putting those birds there at point blank range is the proof that you've done everything absolutely right. You've bent their will; your actions and your decisions put you in control of their destiny! Your attention to detail, your knowledge of the birds and their habits, your ability to "think like a duck" have all been taken to the extreme.

The Right Decoy For The Job

It's impossible, even for the most extreme of us, to make a decoy spread look *too natural*. It is *possible,* using the technology and equipment available to today's waterfowl hunter, to make a spread look *more enticing* than real birds! Selection and, more importantly, proper use of various types of decoys can make it happen. Attraction or "pulling power" is the Holy Grail of the extreme decoy strategist.

A wide variety of decoy designs and materials are available to the modern waterfowl hunter. It seems like every extreme waterfowler has come up with at least one "sure-fire" decoy design during his or her hunting career. Though the percentage of these "greatest ever fakes" that are ever marketed is probably minuscule, enough new designs hit the sporting goods stores every year to leave a hunter's head spinning. Some are truly a better mouse trap, others work as good as anything out there and others seem to attract hunters a lot better than they do ducks or geese.

Usually, creating a spread that looks as good or better than real will rely on combining a number of decoy types and strategies. After all, the only time all of the birds in a flock are doing precisely the same thing is when they're spooked.

Since the pursuit of experiences is what extreme waterfowl hunting is about, we'll all hunt a variety of locations and under widely varied conditions for every legal species of waterfowl. That also means using a wide variety of decoys and decoying strategies.

Even if most of your hunting is done in precisely the same spot like a leased rice field blind, or if you hunt in heavily pressured public areas, you need a variety of decoys and strategies. Continual changes to the spread as the season progresses ensure it's different from what the birds saw the day before or in the next field. It forestalls, if not prevents, them from becoming spread-shy.

Steve Burke, NAHC President, chose the right decoys and set the right spread in this Manitoba wheat field.

For those reasons, as well as the extreme waterfowler's ceaseless quest to have "the best," it pays to have a comprehensive view of decoy types and designs and the best ways to use them.

Decoys For Every Situation

If a decoy's on the market, somebody had to believe there was a use for it. They had to test it, and if they actually hope to sell other hunters on it, we can assume they had a successful hunt or two over it. So that's why decoys for all types of waterfowling come in so many designs and materials. They all offer advantages and disadvantages, and they all have their best uses.

Perhaps you'll face some new waterfowl hunting challenges this season, or maybe you want to just throw a "new look" at the birds in your usual hunting area. Consider these recommendations before making your next decoy purchase or pulling out the spread from the garage attic.

FLOATING DUCK DECOYS
Decoy Type
- Recommended Uses
- *Advantages*
- Disadvantages

Standard Size Or Magnum Weighted Keel Cork, Burlap-Wrapped Urethane, Cedar or other solid type decoys
- Big water hunting where large boat and/or specialized decoys skiff can be used to transport and set decoys.
- *Ride the water most naturally of all types of decoys; bullet-proof—they can absorb multiple pellet hits without noticeable effect on attitude in water or paint scheme; magnums in particular can be seen at great distances; easy to turn heads and otherwise customize; may be self-righting depending on keel design; high nostalgia factor.*
- Expensive—cork or burlap-wrapped decoys can cost $20 apiece or more; feather and paint schemes are least realistic in detail; extremely bulky and heavy to transport and store.

Standard Size Weighted Keel Plastic
- All around use; especially good where birds don't need to spot decoys from a great distance such as flooded timber

hunting; also good for open water hunting with wind and waves; any situation where lots of decoys are needed but space is at a premium.

- *Inexpensive; compact; ride rough water better than aqua keel decoys; wide variety of species available; self-righting.*
- Low visibility on big water unless used in large numbers; heavier than aqua keel decoys; paint may come off with rough handling; will fill with water and sink when sprayed with shot.

Magnum Weighted Keel Plastic

- Best all-around size for wide variety of water types; best for widest range of water and wind.
- *Good visibility on big water; size can make up for smaller number of total decoys in spread; moderately priced; self-righting.*
- Bulky; heavy; difficult to transport in quantity to remote hunting locations, especially if decoys must be carried in by hunter or on a hand cart; will fill with water and sink when sprayed with shot.

On larger bodies of water, weighted keel dekes are best because they ride well even in the wind and waves.

When packing into secluded ponds that the wind doesn't whip up, weight of the decoys is the most important consideration.

Super-Magnum Weighted Keel Plastic
- Big water hunting applications such as reservoirs, tidal flats and ocean hunting; also used to set highly attractive spread on small water using fewest possible decoys.
- *Best visibility in all water, wave and light conditions; most visible type of decoys even at low angles as viewed by diver and sea duck species which tend to fly close to water.*
- Heavy; cumbersome; expensive; special accommodations such as extremely large boat or specialized decoy skiff must be used to transport a large spread; will fill with water and sink when sprayed with shot.

Standard Size Aqua Keel Plastic
- All-around hunting in water situations where decoys don't have to ride waves; good for foot-accessible-only hunting areas.
- *Inexpensive; lightweight; easy carrying to remote hunting locations; offer lifelike motion in light breeze.*
- Low visibility in big water; don't ride rough water with natural appearance; tend to tip over at top of large waves; do not self-right; will fill with water and list or sink when sprayed with shot.

Magnum Aqua Keel Plastic
- Good second choice for hunting secluded areas of larger water or setting attractive spread of few decoys out of heavy wind.
- *Inexpensive; lightweight; easy carrying to remote hunting locations; offer lifelike motion in light breeze; larger size can offer equal or better attraction to more decoys of smaller size.*
- Don't ride rough water with natural appearance; tend to tip over at top of large waves; do not self-right; will fill with water and list or sink when sprayed with shot.

Inflatable, Collapsible or Crushable Floating Decoys
- Remote, wading-accessible-only locations.
- *Inexpensive; extremely lightweight and compact—a dozen are transportable in a standard game pouch on hunting coat; minimal anchors required.*
- Will tip over in light winds; not self-righting; ride water poorly except in lightest breezes; usually not extremely detailed or durable.

FIELD DUCK DECOYS
Decoy Type
- Recommended Uses
- *Advantages*
- Disadvantages

Full-bodied Decoys
- Field spreads for ducks or set off to one side of goose spread; especially useful in areas of taller cover like wheat or barley stubble or picked cornfields where stalks are still in field; also extremely useful on sandbars and rocks submerged in an inch or two of water.
- *Incredible realism and attractiveness to ducks; multiple positions available; add exquisite natural detail when used along shoreline or in extremely shallow water in concert with floating decoys; highly visible even in taller cover; extremely lightweight for size.*
- Bulky; difficult to store or transport large numbers; need to be staked down in gusty winds; expensive; available only in mallard models.

Shell Decoys
- Field hunting situations with low cover; can be used for duck spread or in conjunction with goose spread.
- *Lightweight and nestable; easy to transport large quantities even in foot-accessible-only areas; compact for storage, especially those with removable heads; heads moveable to customize spread; several species available.*
- Poor visibility even in moderate height cover; even when staked, all bodies have same attitude whether head/neck is feeding or resting style; tend to blow over in moderate wind if not staked or "pushed down" into cover, further reducing visibility.

Silhouette Decoys
- Useful in enlarging overall duck spread of shells or full-bodies or in conjunction with goose spread; also useful in situations where ducks will be approaching hunters from over a nearby

This exaggerated view of what a flying bird would see when viewing the various types of field decoys head-on from a low angle reveals why full-body decoys are the most effective.

hill or ridge; can also add realism when used in shallow water or along shoreline near floating duck spread.
- *Inexpensive; many decoys can be easily transported to remote hunting locations; low maintenance; quick to set up; simply painted, even just black silhouettes can be effective in some situations.*
- None commercially available; homemade decoys tend to lack photographic realism; tend to disappear as birds move away from perpendicular viewing angles or are right over top of spread.

Flat Or Dorsal View Decoys
- Should only be used to enlarge spreads of other types of field duck decoys.
- *Inexpensive; lightweight, many can be carried easily to remote hunting location; commercially available with photographic printing processes.*
- Blow away easily unless staked down; no upright silhouette to be visible from distance; only noticed by birds directly overhead.

FLOATING GOOSE DECOYS
Decoy Type
- Recommended Uses
- *Advantages*
- Disadvantages

Standard Size Or Magnum Weighted Keel Cork, Burlap-Wrapped Urethane, Cedar or other solid type decoys
- Big water hunting where large boat and/or specialized decoys skiff can be used to transport and set decoys.
- *Ride the water most naturally of all types of decoys; bullet-proof—they can absorb multiple pellet hits without noticeable effect on attitude in water or paint scheme; magnums in particular can be seen at great distances; usually easy to turn heads and otherwise customize; may be self-righting depending on keel design; high nostalgia factor.*

- Incredibly expensive—cork or burlap-wrapped decoys can cost $40 apiece or more; feather and paint schemes are usually least realistic in detail; extremely bulky and heavy to transport; only for use when a separate decoy skiff is available.

The result of selecting the right decoys and deploying them properly is a good reason to smile.

A few field shells along the shoreline or even in shallow water can make an enticing spread of floaters even more realisitic and deadly!

Standard And Magnum Size Weighted Keel Plastic
- All around use; good for open water hunting with wind and waves.
- *Ride rough water better than most aqua keel decoys; wide variety of species available; self-righting; models with removable heads offer easier transport, storage and customization; most types come with several head/neck attitudes.*
- Bulky; difficult to store or transport large quantities with fixed head; usually require heavy or "gripping" type anchors; will fill with water and sink when sprayed with shot.

Standard And Magnum Size Aqua Keel Plastic
- All-around hunting in water situations where decoys don't have to ride waves; good for foot-accessible-only hunting areas.
- *Inexpensive; lightweight; easier to carry to remote hunting locations; offer lifelike motion in light breeze; excellent to add realism to water near field spread.*
- Bulky; difficult to store or transport large quantities with fixed head; usually require heavy or "gripping" type anchors; will fill with water and sink or list when sprayed with shot.

FIELD GOOSE DECOYS
Decoy Type
- Recommended Uses
- *Advantages*
- Disadvantages

Stuffers
- Commercial hunting operations with "permanent" blinds to which large decoy trailer can be pulled to spread location.
- *Since stuffers are real, taxidermied birds, nothing could be more realistic; each bird is a custom mount so decoys can have an infinite number of lifelike positions and body attitude appropriate to head and neck position.*
- Extremely expensive; high maintenance; low durability; possible legal problems with having hundreds of mounts, probably shot by others; require custom-built trailers for transportation and storage.

Full-Bodied Decoys
- Field hunting spreads where truck or trailer can be driven to hunting location; small numbers also work well in concert with floating decoys when hunting river sand bars for geese.
- *Most realistic of plastic decoys; large size and tall profile are highly visible from all angles; easy to set; numerous head positions available; some models have body attitudes appropriate to head/neck position.*
- Expensive; bulky to transport and store; if heads and necks are removed between uses, they can be time-consuming to reassemble and set; transportation of large spread requires special accommodations.

Super Magnum Shells
- Best size for all-around field hunting.
- *Size makes them highly visible without the erect posture of full-body decoys; fewer decoys offer same pulling power as larger spread of smaller dekes; most effective at hiding hunters, dogs, gear among decoys; all goose species available.*

Yes, those shells are big, but they are what's needed to pull birds from great distances across the wide open prairie.

- Expensive; though they nest together, they are still bulky to transport and store; body attitude the same for all head/neck positions.

Magnum Shells
- Good size for general field hunting.
- *Moderately priced; stackable for easier storage and transport; multiple head positions available; all goose species available.*
- Can blow over in stronger winds unless staked; still bulky and moderately heavy for transport and storage; body attitude same for all head/neck positions.

Standard-Size Shells
- General field hunting with large spread.
- *Easiest to transport and store of shell-type; economical when numbers are more important than size; all goose species available; multiple head/neck positions available.*
- Blow over easily in wind unless staked; body attitude same for all head/neck positions; least pulling power because of reduced visibility due to smaller size.

Farm Form "Cones"
- Excellent for general field hunting in large spread; alone or with other types of decoys.
- *Moderate price; good profile and three dimensionality; have lifelike "waddle" in breeze to windy conditions; nest well so large numbers easy to transport and store.*
- Plastic stakes (part of head) difficult to put in frozen ground; only two head positions available; low or no detail of feathers; body-shape not true to real birds.

Silhouettes
- Field hunting from large spreads; best used in conjunction with other types of field decoys; also useful in hunting river sand bars in concert with floating spread.
- *Inexpensive; modern photo image printing makes them incredibly lifelike when viewed from low angles; durable, lightweight; many decoys easily transportable to remote hunting locations; variety of head/positions and body attitudes now available.*
- Disappear from sight as viewing angle departs from perpendicular; decoys disappear when viewed from front, back or overhead; most homemade models lack detail.

Silhouettes work best toward the center of the spread and clustered tightly around the blinds.

Windsocks

- General field hunting; especially good combined with full-bodies, shells and rags.
- *In breezy to windy conditions, they impart motion to the spread; can be set up quickly; compact for transport and storage; lightweight; self-adjust to wind shift; moderately priced.*
- Look very unnatural under still conditions; low pulling power unless there's enough wind to puff out the sock; high maintenance because of sometimes weak wood or plastic components.

Texas Rag Decoys

- Field hunting with large spread; good in combination with shells, full bodies and/or wind socks.
- *Inexpensive; available in all goose species; versatile in that they can be draped over stubble or tied up on dowel stakes as inexpensive wind socks; definite champion when it comes to transporting huge spreads to remote hunting locations; good motion in light breeze, still okay under calm conditions.*
- Not extremely durable, expect one or two seasons of hard use; difficult to keep clean; blow away easily unless staked; do not come "pre-tied" so they require some assembly.

Flat Or Dorsal View Decoys

- Should only be used to enlarge spreads of other types of field goose decoys.
- *Inexpensive; lightweight, many can be carried easily to remote hunting location; commercially available with photographic printing processes; some have two different species printed on reverse sides.*
- Blow away easily unless staked down; no upright silhouette to be visible from distance; only noticed by birds directly overhead.

FLYING DECOYS
Decoy Type
- Recommended Uses
- *Advantages*
- Disadvantages

Full-Bodied Flyers
- Add pulling power to field and water spreads for ducks and/or geese.
- *Most realistic profile; durable; can be used over water.*
- Expensive; can require fairly stout pole for support so it can be visible to incoming birds; unnatural motion in strong winds; models with removable wings tend to lose wings in wind; difficult to set or retrieve in water situations.

Goose Kites
- Most commonly used in conjunction with huge spreads of Texas rags.
- *Altitude adjustable; some lifelike flying motion added to spread; no support visible to incoming birds.*
- Useless in calm conditions; fussy to keep flying; maintenance intensive; not practical for use over water.

Sometimes the only way to get shooting at spread-wary birds is to move some distance outside of the actual decoy spread.

"Flying decoys" do a terrific job of adding height and motion to spread. Deployed as these are, you can create an incredibly realistic illusion of landing birds.

Goose Magnets
- Terrific addition to any field goose hunting spread.
- *Add unbelievably lifelike motion to a field spread of goose decoys in breeze to moderate wind; still look good in calm conditions; take down into very compact, light package for easy transport and storage of hundreds of decoys.*
- Expensive; time consuming to set up; durable but don't take rough handling well; require study and experience to incorporate properly into spread; not practical for use over water.

Wingers or Dorsal View Flyers
- In conjunction with other decoys in field or water spread.
- *Inexpensive; easy to set; can impart some motion to spread.*
- Poor detail; birds have poor depth perception so they have a hard time telling decoy is not laying on the ground; strong wind plays havoc with position and realism.

New Movement In Decoying Ducks & Geese

It was a long time ago; so long ago in fact, that my best hunting friend Mike Boeselager and I were out of school on a Friday because the teachers were at their annual late-October convention. So long ago that Mike and I rousted his mom out of bed in the wee hours of the morning to drive us to the locally-famed Sheboygan Marsh because we weren't yet old enough to drive. So long ago that we had enough ambition to break some pretty heavy sheet ice for the entire mile-long paddle out to "the best" spot on the public hunting area.

I remember we learned that morning that the best way to break the ice with a canoe was to get up a head of steam so the bow would lunge up on the ice sheet, then bounce on the bottom of the canoe to break through, then reach out with the push pole and break as much as we could around us. Then, back off and do it again. Needless to say, the going was slow. When we reached sections of the channel where the current was slower and the ice was thicker, Mike would get out on to the shore and pull the canoe with a rope while I chopped ice with the paddle and push pole. Despite temperatures in the 20s, we were both sweating like crazy! Some might have called us stubborn; some might have called us crazy, but even then we were two extreme waterfowlers bound and determined to reach the "lake" where there'd be enough open water to float our decoys.

We would have liked to have been there before legal shooting light, but that wasn't to be. Legal shooting, then full sunrise, found us still struggling up the channel. As the ducks began to fly to and from feeding, many small flocks of the northern flight mallards buzzed the canoe and its two voyageurs who had now stripped down to their white T-shirts to finish the struggle. As focused as our middle-school minds were on reaching the lake, what was happening didn't register at first, but looking back over the years, there was only one thing that could have been pulling those birds to look at us—motion.

Not to leave you hanging, we did make it to our hard-earned destination on the lake about an hour after sunrise. Though our youthful shooting skills kept us well short of a limit under the old "point system" bag limits of the '70s, Mike and I were witness to a flight of Canadian "red-legged" mallards that any waterfowl hunter is lucky to witness a few times in a lifetime of hunting. The birds were there, a lot of their preferred backwater haunts were frozen up tight, and they were looking for company!

Much more recently, I witnessed the allure of motion on a small pothole in the Parklands of Alberta. Again we were after mallards, but this time on the front side of October. And again, the birds were thick.

Our outfitter, Kevin Rolff of Bittern Lake Lodge, helped us select a promising slough from the thousands that dot this region, which is truly the border between Alberta's farmlands and its northwoods. The mallards had poured into this cattail-shrouded puddle by the hundreds the evening before we went to hunt it.

As we hiked across the barley stubble to reach the slough in the center of the section, a few mosquitoes buzzed us. The air was warm and still. In fact, there wasn't the hint of a breeze.

The open water in the slough was small and particularly narrow. It was a challenge to toss a dozen and a half dekes on it and still leave an attractive opening in the spread for the ducks to key on. The cattails swallowed up each of us three hunters as we sat on buckets just six feet back from the water's edge. We couldn't have built better blinds if we would have had the inclination.

As expected, ducks started swinging by the slough late in the afternoon.

The season was a couple of weeks old, but this slough had not been hunted. Yet the birds acted like demons had possessed this Alberta Parkland pothole. They wouldn't come closer than 60 yards no matter how sweetly or demandingly we called. They were having none of it.

After a number of flocks acted like our little slough was quarantined, our group of hunters met at the end of the pond. We looked over the spread; we looked at each of us sitting in his "blind." We walked the perimeter of the slough looking for a fertilizer bag that might have blown in across the fields. We even glassed the surrounding field for coyotes or anything else that might be spooking the ducks. We found nothing.

We considered trying to lie down out in the field some distance from the slough and shooting the ducks as they made their long-range pass—a trick that Texas goose hunters often use when the sun crests the horizon and decoy-shy birds flare from white spreads at long distances. Yet the birds we had seen piling into the pond just the night before told us they should be decoying.

We looked at the pond again. Our 18 decoys sat there reflected as in a mirror on the surface of the pothole. It was a beautiful scene—except—it didn't look real! Those ducks should be kicking up a fuss enjoying the bounty of safe water so close to feed! Ah ha!

I dug through my usually well-supplied blind bag only to find I didn't have along the usual 50 feet of parachute cord we could have used to set up a splasher rig. What to do? One of my companions went out into the shallow pond and stomped around until the water was good and muddied up, the way feeding ducks would have it. I picked up the bucket I had been sitting on and filled it with water. Then I slung the water as far as I could out into the pond. The disturbance made the decoys bob and weave a bit. Could it possibly work?

For the rest of the time until the end of legal shooting, we rotated turns as the bucket brigade. One hunter would be the gunner, two stood by with pails of water at the ready. When a bird was spotted at a medium distance, the first bucketeer would pitch a pail full on the pond. As they got closer, the second would kind of spread his pail of water low over the surface.

That's all it took. The ducks saw the ripples. They saw the decoys move. They saw the roiled water. And they came in.

With the number of ducks on the Alberta Parklands that fall, we could have shot a truck load. Instead, each of us took what we wanted, short of legal limits, and then sat back to watch the spectacle and reflect on the lessons of the afternoon.

Note how much bigger magnum decoys are than the real birds. It's believed they work because ducks and geese have terrific eyesight but poor depth perception.

My own personal tales of motion attracting birds could fill an entire book. I've seen it work in duck and goose spreads in almost every place I've hunted. Replicated natural movement of the decoys and the water are among the most critical elements in boosting the pulling power of any decoy spread.

Whether birds are feeding in a field or resting on the water, ducks and geese don't just plop out of the sky and become statues. They are a blur of motion. They fight for choice morsels, they preen, they look around for danger, they tip up to feed, they dive, they stretch their wings.

Taking an afternoon tour of the non-hunting portion of the Grey Lodge Management Area in California's Butte Sink region left an incredible impression on me. Hundreds of thousands of teal, pintails, mallards, gadwall, widgeon and more winter in this area. The small area we could see had tens of thousands of birds on it in our view at one time.

Watching the ducks in the bright sun was almost like "seeing stars" when I try to straighten out the duck boat full of decoys on its trailer by myself. Almost constantly among the dark silhouettes of the mass of ducks were dozens of flashes of white. They were birds rearing back on the water and stretching their wings. Seeing that, it was easy to understand how easily the sharp-eyed flying birds can key in on flocks on the ground from great distances!

Making Them Move

Adding movement to your decoy spreads isn't difficult. You simply need to analyze the type of movement necessary to make your decoy spread "become" a flock of real birds.

For example, on open water or in an open field, the wind will give some types of decoys lifelike movement. Floating puddle duck decoys, properly tethered with the anchor line running through the front hole on the keel, will appear to swim somewhat in a light breeze or gusting winds. Yet they will keep the spread oriented facing the wind which is natural for waterfowl.

Wind is relied upon in the design of some field decoys like windsocks. Even a slight breeze will billow out these decoys and orient them into the wind. Fluctuations in the flow of the wind give them lifelike motion. The Farm Form Decoy, which is a cone shaped variation of the traditional full-bodied decoy, uses the wind to produce a very realistic waddle. Though they don't actually move forward, when viewed from a distance, a properly set spread of Farm Forms looks like a flock of real geese waddling into the wind as they feed.

Wind even adds a lifelike ripple to traditional rag decoys or their modern variants like the Texas Hunting Products Sheet-Dec. Rag decoys are very versatile and can be tied up into a number of variations with or without dowels to stake them down. The only drawback to rags traditionally laid on the ground is their low profile and the fact that wind can blow them away! Texas Hunting Products Sheet Decs are available in snow, blue and light goose models.

Unfortunately, wind is a fickle thing. It seems like it's either not blowing or blowing too hard just when we want the "right" amount of wind to impart motion to our decoys. Several situations in puddle duck hunting in particular, preclude the use of wind as the generator of decoy motion.

For example, flooded timber hunting and hunting small, woodland potholes or sloughs hide you and the ducks from the brunt of the wind. That's often what makes those places alluring to the hunters and the hunted!

Arkansas is probably most famous for flooded timber hunting. There, duck guides have been imparting motion to their decoys simply by splashing around in the water.

Successful timber hunters rely more upon their setup to sound like real birds than to look realistic because by the time the flock of real birds actually see the decoys, they are already pretty much committed. Having the decoys out is mostly to give the birds what they expected to see when they broke through the tree tops. That's why big, loud calling plays such an important role in this type of hunting.

However, one of timber hunting's subtleties is to splash the surface of the water with your hand, foot or paddle. Not only does this make the sounds like a bunch of acorn frenzied mallards splashing and dabbling beneath the timber canopy, but it also creates radiating rings of surface disturbance like that caused by real ducks. While the anchored decoys stay in one place, these rings radiate out around the spread, catching the light as they move below the openings in the treetops. Ducks that might otherwise miss the location of the spread because of the density of the timber can home in on the source of these wavelets. Those moving, concentric ripples will be found wherever ducks are active on the water and appear entirely natural to the flying ducks.

Attention to detail in the spread, down to precise placement of each block on the water (rather than pitching decoys hither and yon) is the sign of an extreme waterfowl hunter.

When you're hunting a small pond or slough, or anytime the wind isn't helping to move the decoys, you can add movement by creating these wave rings. The system can be as simple as carrying a pocketful of stones to your hunting area and flipping them out into the decoys when an interested flock's attention is focused elsewhere. It doesn't sound very sophisticated and it isn't, but it does work. The drawbacks are ducks spotting you throwing at the wrong time, making sure the dog knows this isn't retrieving practice and taking the chance that uninitiated hunters will tell stories back at the club about the nut who was chuckin' rocks at his own decoys.

Another way to create this kind of motion in your decoys is to set up your own simple splasher system.

After all the other decoys are set, run a 50- to 80-foot length of dark-colored cord with a small snap on one end through the eye of an anchor weighing a couple of pounds or better. Lock the dull finished snap in place on the anchor line hole on the weighted keel of a flip-tail feeder style decoy. With the decoy in one hand and the spool of cord in the other, lower the anchor slowly to the bottom while trying to avoid tangling the line in any weeds.

Plop the decoy gently on the water over the anchor and slowly back away toward your blind while allowing the necessary amount of line to roll off the spool.

Test the splasher by pulling gently on the cord to see that it creates an up and down motion on the flip-tail and isn't tangled in the weeds. Then slowly continue toward your blind. Be careful that the cord doesn't foul any of the anchor lines holding the decoys you've already set.

From the blind you'll be able to jiggle and bounce the fliptail as much as you like, creating movement in all the decoys more similar to those of real ducks.

You can make this type of system as elaborate as you want by adding more splashers or creating a custom splasher like a full-bodied floating decoy which can sit on the water or tip up like a flip-tail feeder.

One more hint is to have the blind end of the cord actually attached to the spool and make the spool of something that floats. Then even if the spool is dropped in the excitement of calling and shooting, it can be found quickly and the anchor won't be lost.

Higdon Motion Decoys Systems has taken the principle of the splasher system to a whole new level in both field and floating

The flexible neck on this Higdon decoy allows you to build incredibly lifelike motion into your field spread.

decoys. For field goose hunters, Higdon has developed head and neck systems for full-bodied decoys that feed, preen, look around and shake with incredibly lifelike motions when the cord is pulled. For commercial operations where setup isn't a concern, they even have a motorized cam system to operate many moving decoys at once and as continually as you'd like without wearing out your arms! The Higdon water unit is an automatic "splasher" decoy called "Jack The Rippler," which sets up a steady, natural motion in the entire spread!

A variety of motorized decoys are also available to add motion to your water spreads. Some simply use a propeller to create the same kind of motion as the splasher rig while anchored in one spot. There are also elaborate, radio-controlled models that will swim throughout the rig under your control. Cost is the major disadvantage on these decoys, with radio-controlled models running up to several hundred dollars. And for those of us who have problems with microwave ovens and VCRs, trying to run a radio-controlled decoy while looking for birds, calling and shooting could prove to be a whole new extreme waterfowling challenge!

Recreating Wing Stretching

Though it's not very old, the most well-known recreation of landing birds and wing stretching among birds already on the ground is the technique known as flagging. It's rumored this technique was originally developed in the "glory days" of goose hunting on Maryland's Eastern Shore. Canada geese migrating through and wintering in this area were hunted hard and quickly became spread shy. Commercial hunting operations in this area made use of every legal decoying technique to bring birds in for their hunters. Most ended up going to the extreme of using huge spreads of stuffer decoys—actual taxidermied birds.

Even with such enviable realism at their disposal, the key element of motion was missing. Thus flagging was born.

Flagging or winging on the most basic level is simply waving a flag or a pair of paddles to attract the attention of distant birds. For Canada geese the flags are usually black or dark gray.

Randy Bartz is the Flag Man. His T-Flags and the techniques he has pioneered have been huge leaps forward for extremists looking for lifelike decoy spreads.

Flagging techniques can be as varied as the hunters performing this extreme waterfowler's semaphore. Some guides only flag until a distant flock has been turned toward the spread. Others have had great success flagging the birds right into shotgun range. Some say the flagging should be done at ground level, just above the edge of the pit blind in the middle of the decoys. Other will stand up and flag from the edge of the spread. Some will stand tall and flag above their heads until the birds are coming in, then slowly lower the flapping paddles until they are crouching and the paddles are just moving above the ground.

A long pole with a flag creates an even more realistic illusion.

The man who has done more to perfect flagging equipment and techniques than anyone else is NAHC Member Randy Bartz of Oronoco, Minnesota. Randy hunts and guides hunters for waterfowl all over North America each fall. During the few months of "off season," Randy trains extreme retrievers and manages his company, quite appropriately called Flagman Products. Randy Bartz is the Flag Man.

Randy has created goose flags for snow and Canada goose hunting that quite logically are shaped like geese. They're called T-Flags, and they are extremely versatile. One version can be used to flap on a short stick much like the traditional roots of flagging. Other versions can be used on long poles to recreate birds landing in the spread. The newest one actually attaches to the bottom of a hunter's shotgun barrel so that when he sits up from his hiding spot among the decoys to shoot, the incoming birds will think it's just a bird on the ground flapping its wings and will continue to come in! Until you've seen Flagman flags in use in a spread from a distance and you've seen them pull birds, you can't fully appreciate the pulling power they have.

Another way to impart wing-stretching appeal to a spread is to incorporate some of the new wing attachments into your rig. These are simply plastic or framed-fabric wings that clip onto the backs of standard or full-bodied decoys. Though they don't actually move on their own, the breeze can impart some motion to them. The effect offers better realism than a set with no spread wings.

Just a crossed pair of flags on a decoy's back can add a great deal of lifelike motion and enhance the eye-catching illusion of birds stretching their wings.

Decoying On A New Level

Next to motion, the most important characteristic to give a decoy spread is depth, or layers. Traditional water and field spreads are very two-dimensional. They have length and width, but they have very little height.

Shell and standard floating decoys sit low to the ground and water. Some designs of floating decoys have all the heads set in a resting position, tucked low to the body. They make for a very "low profile" spread. Goose decoys tend to be taller because of the birds' long necks, but extreme waterfowlers know the spread should be set with no more than one erect, sentinel head to every four or five resting and feeding heads. The biggest problem with shell goose decoys is that they are designed to have the flat underside sitting on the ground. That makes a spread look like a field full of birds sitting on nests and not very natural.

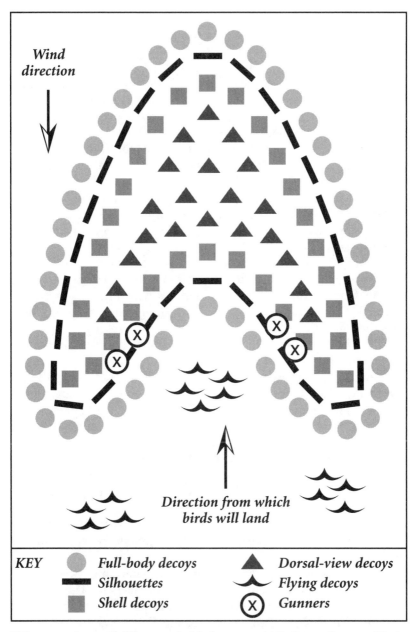

Wind direction

Direction from which birds will land

KEY			
⬤	*Full-body decoys*	▲	*Dorsal-view decoys*
▬	*Silhouettes*	〰	*Flying decoys*
▪	*Shell decoys*	Ⓧ	*Gunners*

When setting a field spread, it's best to work from the outside in forming annular rings of decoys. The "tallest" decoys should be on the outside working toward the middle with the lowest decoys.

So the first level toward better realism is the use of full-bodied decoys. Flambeau, Big Foot, Carry-Lite, G&H and others are manufacturing these most lifelike of all molded plastic goose decoys. Flambeau has added an extremely realistic "Enticer" line of full-bodied mallards as well. An extreme waterfowl hunter with an imaginative eye can immediately see how these truly 3-D decoys can boost the appearance of the spread.

To combine full-bodies with shells, or any type of decoys for that matter, put your most three-dimensional decoys on the outline of the spread and work your way toward the center to the least three-dimensional. Full-bodies and windsocks (if there's enough breeze to billow them) will form the outline of the spread. Inside of them go the shells; inside of them are the rags and silhouettes mixed with the dorsal view dekes.

In combination with a goose spread, some Enticers set off to one side or as a small pod at the top of the goose spread landing area will suck in field-feeding mallards, sometimes with little or no calling required. Ducks that used to just buzz the goose spread will now have their feet down for landing!

Full-bodied decoys also add realism along the shoreline near a water setup, or even better, standing in water an inch or two deep.

Viewed from almost any range, getting as many decoys as possible "up on their feet" takes realism from the good level to the great level, but there's more you can do: Add flying decoys to your spread.

Several types of flying decoys are available to extreme waterfowl hunters. The first is the full-bodied molded plastic version. Some are one-piece units, others have detachable wings. They are placed out in the field, marsh or lake on fiberglass or metal poles stuck in the ground or mud. For the most drawing power, use several in a V-formation with the front bird just above the water or stubble and the back birds 15 or 20 feet in the air. The new heights to which you'll take your spread depend on how much conduit you're willing to tote to your hunting area!

Goose Magnet decoys are sort of a combination between a kite and a goose-shape flag suspended on top of a pole. Their special design created by North American Hunting Club member and extreme waterfowler Tim Peterson actually allows them to flap their wings in a breeze! The motion is so lifelike, I've found myself dropping to the stubble when I've viewed them from a distance. I was certain birds were landing in the spread with my hunting buddies, and I didn't want to spook them! That's how real the motion is! Goose Magnets are small, light and very compact, so adding large quantities to your rig won't add much of a transportation headache.

Feather Flex offers what it calls "Wingers." These are dorsal view silhouettes of flying ducks and geese that are placed on poles like full-bodied flying decoys. Waterfowl flying overhead see these as birds flying at a lower altitude; however, when viewed from the lower angle of decoying birds, they tend to disappear—the downfall of any silhouette type decoy.

There are also kites designed to look like flying geese. These are often used in conjunction with huge white spreads for snow geese and by sophisticated commercial hunting operations for Canada geese. When combined with a large, well-set field spread, kites can be deadly on all types of geese. They offer the advantage of being light and compact, yet allow you to set the flying decoys at heights much greater than is practical to place full-bodied decoys on poles.

Besides creating a three-dimensional appearance in the spread, kite decoys can be used as great range and elevation markers for taking incoming birds. Texas guides sometimes set a decoy for a first-time hunter and tell him not to shoot unless the bird is closer than the kite ... and don't shoot the kite!

The key to using any type of flying decoy is knowing how to place it properly. At first thought, it's logical that the best place for them is in or approaching the landing area you've set up in the decoys. That's where you're trying to get the birds to land.

In practice, this can create a problem. It seems to "stall out" incoming birds when they are just out of good shooting range. They see these landing birds and to avoid mid-air collisions, they want to wait until the birds in front of them are on the ground. The problem is the decoys never land, so the real geese never come any closer.

To counteract this effect, there are two good options. The best is to place your flying decoys ahead of the landing area, some inside the spread, some in small groups outside the spread. This way the birds will see a clear path to the landing zone you've built and positioned the shooters near. The second option is to position the flyers in the landing area as seems most natural, then move the hunters 50 to 100 yards downwind of the spread, where chances are the "stalled" birds will be hovering right above them.

Silhouettes Have Come A Long Way

For years, silhouettes didn't get a lot of respect, especially from waterfowl hunters who do most of their hunting for heavily pressured birds. Guys who used a spread of primarily or exclusively silhouettes were pitied by other hunters. The philosophy was: "That must be all they can afford."

In those days when most silhouettes were homemade from cardboard or plywood or Masonite, they ended up being either not too durable or as heavy as shell decoys. Plastics changed that.

Homemade decoys seldom had much detail. Painting was usually done with spray paint. A revolution in the way printing could be done on plastics and in utilizing photographic images to develop the patterns changed that.

Historically, silhouettes have the disadvantage of disappearing to the birds when viewed from either end or directly above. As far as true silhouette decoys go, that hasn't changed. However, a better understanding of how to use and position silhouettes has minimized that problem. And at least one manufacturer has come up with a new design to help eliminate that problem altogether.

The premier names in silhouette decoys today are Outlaw, Real Geese and Flambeau. Each of these companies produces highly durable silhouettes which have photo-realistic images. When viewed broadside, it's difficult to tell that they are not 3-dimensional. That was always the gripe, "They look flat." Old, painted silhouettes looked like paintings. Photo realistic silhouettes look like geese.

Traditionally, silhouette decoys were produced in a couple of very "stiff" positions—feeding and alert. Because the new generation silhouettes are produced from photos of geese, they can be in as many positions as the manufacturer is willing to produce dies for! Flambeau's new "Imposter" silhouettes come in six different positions to the dozen!

A new decoy manufacturer called North-East Decoys out of Quebec, Canada is also striving for a more 3-D appearance in silhouettes but is taking a different tack. North-East decoys are covered with a patent pending non-glare, permanent velvet finish. Viewed at a distance under any light condition, the velvet finish gives the birds, particularly in the head and neck area, a rounded, 3-dimensional appearance. Four neck postures are available to promote the illusion of action and the necks swivel back against the body for durability and added customization in the spread.

To help reduce the problem of the decoys disappearing when viewed from overhead, the "3-D" North-East model has fold down sides also finished with the special velvet process. Because of the illusion of "roundness" that the velvet gives, the flat fold down sides do a good job of filling out the decoy in the birds' sight.

North-East decoys have a special velvet finish that creates the illusion of roundness, even on the silhouette models.

You can tell the folks at North-East Decoys are extreme waterfowl hunters because of the attention they give to detail. For example, their snow goose decoys have two different shades of velvet covering. One is the typical pure white of a mature snow. The second is a dusty gray brown which perfectly mimics an immature bird. In their own hunting, they mix in the proper percentage of young birds to old birds based on the flyway report on the nesting success and juvenile percentage of the migrating flock!

No matter what type of silhouettes you decide to use, you can also limit the disappearing bird syndrome by positioning the decoys oriented toward the wind but not all facing precisely into the wind. By positioning silhouettes anywhere from zero degrees to 60 degrees either

A spread consisting primarily of silhouettes will need to have birds facing in all directions so the spread doesn't disappear when viewed from any angle.

side of the oncoming wind, you'll maximize the points of the compass from which working birds will see "whole geese." That's valuable information when seeking a natural look from any decoy spread. Ducks and geese will sit oriented into the wind, but they won't all be facing directly into the wind at all times! You can recreate that in your spread by situating birds as much as 45 degrees off the wind direction for 3-D decoys and as much as 60 degrees off the wind for silhouettes. Birds in a flock on the ground do not all face precisely the same direction at the same time unless they are alarmed.

Specialty Decoys

Sometimes one of the best tactics to entice hard-hunted birds is to show them a look that's different from what everyone else is showing them. If everyone else is hunting the middle of the section, try hunting the edge of the section. If everyone else is hunting far from farm buildings, try hunting as close to the buildings as you can get permission to. If everyone else is using huge spreads, try just a few dozen decoys in yours. Don't be afraid to experiment to find success.

One trick that only extreme waterfowl hunters bother to use is putting out confidence decoys. They can be replicas of any species common to the area other than the ones you're hunting. Those commercially available include coot, herons, seagulls, egrets and crows.

Confidence decoys placed in the general vicinity of a spread assure incoming birds that everything is all right. The distance from the spread varies depending on the species of confidence decoy you're using. It might help to place a heron decoy 100 yards from the blind under the anticipated flight path of incoming ducks. It would reduce fears they might have in approaching the spread. Sometimes seagull decoys are placed right on top of a well camouflaged blind. A half-dozen coot placed at the far edge of shotgun range serve as a very natural looking range indicator and tend to keep ducks looking for the natural landing opening you've built into your spread much closer to the blind.

Because of a heron or egret decoy's greater size and brighter coloration, replicas of these species are more easily spotted at a distance by ducks and geese than the small, drably colored duck decoys. In really heavily hunted areas, like public lands in some parts of California, hunters are finding success by wading as far away from the usual hunting haunts as they can, then putting out just a half dozen coot decoys. The presence of just the coot seems to make the late season pintails and mallards feel like nothing could be wrong here because nobody is trying to fool them with a bunch of coot. Who knows—but it works!

The critical factor is selecting confidence decoys that replicate species the ducks are used to seeing. The wrong confidence decoy is worse than none at all because it further alerts already wary birds that something is not right!

Specialty decoys should also be incorporated right into a spread to enhance lifelike appearance. Little details, such as decoys with moveable heads, spell the difference when dealing with wary ducks or geese.

The best spreads will include decoys in a variety of positions. Feeding heads, resting heads, sleeping postures, flip-tail feeders, preening birds and any other natural posture should be incorporated. No one manufacturer offers all that is needed, so some shopping is required. The most extreme waterfowl hunters consider customizing or building their own decoys based on their personal observations of ducks and geese.

Even birds of the same species don't all look exactly alike in a flock. Some are larger; some are smaller. Some are dark; some are light. Especially in the fall, many birds still wear dull, juvenile plumage or stages of eclipse plumage.

Opinions are mixed on mixing sizes of decoys within a spread. We're told the reason magnum decoys work is because ducks and

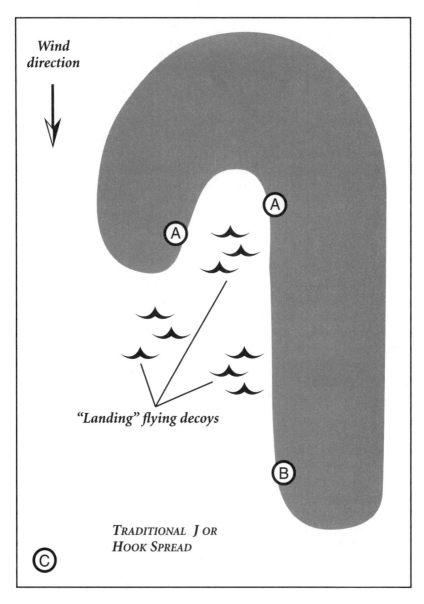

Wind direction

Ⓐ

Ⓐ

"Landing" flying decoys

Ⓑ

TRADITIONAL *J* OR
HOOK SPREAD

Ⓒ

The use of "flying" decoys may change where the gunners are positioned in the spread. The "A" positions would be the traditional gun placement. Location "B" is where the guns may need to be if the birds are "stalling out" behind the fliers. Position "C" is an option for wary birds that are shying from the spread altogether.

geese do not recognize them as oversized. While waterfowl eyesight and color acuity are estimated at least 10 times better than humans, their depth perception is poor. In other words, when they see a magnum decoy, they simply perceive it as a fellow fowl that is closer than it really is.

If this is the case, then mixing drastically different-sized decoys in the same part of the spread may be confusing and appear unnatural to ducks. Because you want to make the ducks and geese believe they understand completely what's going on below them, this could be detrimental to the effectiveness of the spread. So a mix of standard and super magnum decoys can be used in the same spread, but the giant decoys should be segregated from the smaller blocks.

In areas with a mix of duck species, it may be wise to use several species of decoys, too. Though the number of species may all use the same field or resting area, you'll seldom see truly mixed flocks in the air. Even when they land, they tend to segregate and stick with their own. The adage "birds of a feather flock together" is founded in fact.

Geese will also segregate in the same feeding field, and it's amazing how birds will decoy to their own kind within a spread. Even with 1,000 white decoys out for snow geese and 50 Canadas off to one edge of the spread just in case, the dark geese will without fail go to the dark fakes. A half dozen full-bodied mallard decoys in a pod at the top of a landing area in a spread of 1,500 goose decoys will somehow get the attention of mallards flying by. They'll home in on just a couple of their kin among the blanket of white!

A guide knows he's done his job of setting the spread well when his hunters produce a morning like this!

8

The Mystery Of Calling

*E*very extreme waterfowl hunter considers calling to be essential. Each of us regards it as one of the most powerful skills in our bag of tricks to lure ducks and geese into range. Calling is as important as guns, shells, decoys and a good dog, right?

Maybe.

The more we examine why calling attracts or doesn't attract waterfowl, the less we understand about the craft and why it works. One day it appears your simplest calls are siren songs to every bird on the marsh; even sour notes don't phase them. The next day, calling to the same ducks under seemingly the same conditions, you might as well be blowing a tuba for all the good your finest calling does.

As much as we'd like it to be, calling is not the "secret weapon" that will bring birds into range *every* time we go hunting!

That's not just the opinion of a frustrated caller. Even the best in the world will tell you that some days, some ducks are uncallable. Ask Buck Gardner.

Buck was the 1994 World Champion Duck Caller and the 1995 Champion of Champions. (The Champion of Champions contest is held every five years among previous World Champions. The winner goes out on top but agrees never to blow in competition again!)

Buck, owner of Rich N Tone game calls, hunts ducks and geese all over North America every year. Buck's devotion and methods define the phrase "extreme waterfowl hunting."

Buck is the first to admit that contest calling is a whole lot different than blowing for real ducks in timber and rice fields. Yet just ten minutes into an Arkansas mallard hunt in his company will prove to anyone that Buck can sweet-talk real ducks as well as contest judges! A lifetime of extreme waterfowl hunting in some of the best duck country in the world has taught Buck to play the plaintive music big green-heads love to hear.

Even a Champion of Champions caller like Buck Gardner (right) will admit that some days, some ducks are simply uncallable!

Yet every once in a while, the ducks even ignore Buck. He says it's because they didn't get a good look at those championship rings he wears, but when he's serious he'll tell you that sometimes the ducks will not respond to a call ... period.

Well if the World Champion, Champion of Champions extreme waterfowl hunter can't make the ducks come in every time, then what chance does the everyday, run of the mill extreme duck hunter have?

A pretty darn good one. Because on other days, those same ducks will fall for almost anything. The big question is, "Why?"

Why Do Ducks Come To A Call?

That's a darn good question.

In most other game calling like bugling for elk or yelping for spring turkeys or even rattling and grunting for white-tailed deer, you're playing on the mating instinct. Mating is perhaps the most powerful urge of all. When your call either threatens the chance to breed or offers an opportunity to mate, the attractions are easily understood.

In the case of the elk or deer, you're demanding the male to come and fight or risk losing his females. In turkey hunting you're pretending to be the very object of a gobbler's lust!

For most of the waterfowl season in the biggest chunk of North America, calling waterfowl isn't playing on their mating urges. Extreme waterfowl hunters who hunt the wintering areas well into January or even February in the southern U.S. and Mexico do report that calling seems to become more consistently effective later into the season. That may be because the birds are beginning to pair up for the flights back to the nesting grounds. Some of the courtship rituals between prospective mates are vocal.

Elk and turkey calling are also different because in most cases you're getting a direct response from the animal. You call to them, they call back to you. Additionally, when a turkey or an elk calls back to you, it's divulging its location without necessarily being in view. That means, depending on the setup, if the bull or gobbler won't come to you, you might be able to go to it!

With ducks, that only happens with the odd single mallard drake who will grunt back at you or the Suzy in the front of the flock who just has to talk back at your calling. Sometimes widgeon and pintails will whistle back at you. And even if you do get the birds to respond vocally, the intent of waterfowl calling is to make the birds come all the way to you. Usually, there's no opportunity to move in on them.

Geese are usually big talkers! However, most of the time, the duck caller is making decisions on when to blow and what sounds to use based on the experience of watching birds react. The only way to learn what calls to make then is to blow at wild ducks and experiment. So becoming an expert caller takes years and years of in-the-field experience.

It seems a logical guess that in most cases the allure in calling ducks and geese is playing on their propensity to be social. They like to flock because of their natural instinct for safety in numbers, and calling is just an efficient way of assembling the flock. In most cases, it seems that waterfowl calling has no demanding appeal like the struggle to pass on genes to future generations.

As flocking animals, ducks do sound alarm calls to warn the rest of the flock of danger, but those are sounds hunters strive to stay away from. A hen mallard's frantic quacking or a wood duck's alarm squeal can flare birds as fast as wearing a blaze orange coat, sometimes faster!

On the other hand, when waterfowl are content and feeling safe, they'll feel safer when even more birds are around them. As a result, it seems logical to assume that they call to tell passersby how good things are where they are, and that they should come in and enjoy the bounty and safety. Calls that send that invitation are the contented quacks of a hen mallard; the guttural grunts of greenheads; the whistles of widgeon, pintails, teal and wood ducks; the general low rumble of happily feeding ducks and geese. These are the calls extreme waterfowl hunters learn to recreate to perfection and use to great benefit ... on the good days.

So if we make the assumption that the primary reason waterfowl call to one another is simply to attract attention, then that's what we as hunters should be trying to do with our calling—attract attention to our fake ducks in the decoy spread. Once that has been done, the decoys take over the real work of bringing the birds into gun range.

Team calling with each hunter hitting on his strengths can be very effective.

Flooded timber hunters have known this for years. It's the reason Arkansas-style duck calling is loud and long. When hunting timber, extreme waterfowl hunters blow the call almost all the time whether ducks are in sight or not. They are trying to attract the attention of ducks that might be flying above the treetops. In those thick bottoms, sound is about the only way for ducks to know where other ducks are or, in this case, where the spread is located. As soon as the ducks get below the tops of the trees or pass over the opening where the spread is set, the hunters switch primarily to low quacks and feeding jabber. They stick with the softer calling until the guns are going off or until the ducks show signs of leaving or having missed the spread altogether. Then it's time for those crystal clear highballs again to remind the ducks where you are.

The great distance at which ducks can spot each other—or a decoy spread—say, on the prairies of North Dakota, might be part of the reason that timber-style calling seldom works there. It may not seem authentic for ducks to hear such loud calling when they can see the birds that are making the noise.

When you switch to geese, then all the rules, and probably all the motivations for coming to a call, change. They even probably change from goose species to goose species. All that's guaranteed is we'll fully understand why waterfowl respond to calls the day we find a duck or goose that speaks human!

Learning To Call Ducks & Geese

This is a topic we can all agree on. The best way to learn to call ducks and geese is to listen to real ducks and geese! The next best way is to get your hands on some good instruction videos and cassette tapes. Use the expert advice from the world's best callers like Buck Gardner, Sean Mann, Fred Zinc, Eli Haydel, Wil Primos, Brad Harris and many others to develop your basic skills. Then get some recordings of real birds. Listen to the tapes and blow along with them.

Once the pros have taught you the mechanics of making the sounds and you've found some calls you can reliably make those sounds with, then practice, practice, practice. In your vehicle on the way to and from work is a great place to practice. It's private and you won't have an unappreciative spouse asking you to "take that outside" where your neighbors might ask you to "take that inside."

It takes a lot more to impress calling contest judges than it does to call ducks in the field.

Another outstanding way to learn and improve your calling is to seek out your state or regional waterfowl calling club. Many of these organizations are primarily involved in promoting calling contests, but nearly every competitive duck and goose caller started out as a hunter who decided he or she was good enough to compete! Becoming part of their circle is a great way to garner "secrets" to improve your field calling ... maybe even a hunting invitation or two!

Understanding The Reaction

Equally important to learning how to make the sounds of ducks and geese is learning what the different sounds mean and when to use them based on the birds' reaction. Take as an example the basic mallard calls—the highball or greeting call, the come-on-in or come-on-back call and the feeding chuckle. Knowing the sounds is important. Knowing when to use each sound is even more important.

As a primer on which calls to use, imagine a flock of mallards as a bunch of teenagers setting up a Friday night party. The greeting call or highball is loud and long and used to attract ducks' attention from a distance. Think of it as a high-schooler spotting some friends across the crowded, noisy cafeteria at lunch time. "Hey you guys, my folks are gone tonight. You want to come over for pizza?" yells one girl across the crowded lunchroom.

She watches and listens to her friends for their reaction. They obviously didn't hear.

"H-e-e-e-e-y," she nearly screams again, "You guys want to come over for pizza tonight?"

"Yeah, we'll be there at seven!" they shout back.

The come-on-in or come-on-back call consists of medium-level quacks and is used as the ducks approach for a closer look.

As her friends pass closer on their way out of the lunchroom, our young lady fills in some details about the party, "Now you guys bring the drinks, but my dad left money for the pizza. Bring some videos if you want, too. I'll see you about seven."

That's the same excited tone she uses when the friends show up at her door. "Glad you guys are here. *Come on in!*"

The feeding chuckle with an occasional, happy "quack, quack, quack-quack-quack" thrown in is used when the flying ducks are really close to convince them of total safety and contentment.

Back at the party, the pizzas arrive and the young'uns dive into some serious eating. They're laughing and slurping strings of hot mozzarella off their chins. The sounds of joy are only occasionally broken with a "Did you hear who she's going with?" and the odd, "Then I said...then he said..."

The key to being a really successful waterfowl caller is to be able to read the birds and anticipate their reactions to various calls as naturally as it is to picture what those teenagers will do and think. On the other hand, maybe you need to be a whole lot better at duck calling!

Tips To Boost Your Calling Success

Since calling is such an inexact science, the best way to find out what's working or what's not on any particular day is trial and error. If you hit on something that works, keep doing it until it doesn't. If you try something that flares the birds, don't do that again!

For those times when nothing seems to be working, here are some tactics and practice schemes you might have overlooked. What have you got to lose?

Try those other ducky sounds. When the basic mallard highballs, come-back calls and feeding chuckle don't seem to be working, try adding the other sounds ducks make. For example, throw in the half-grunt half-whistle of a drake mallard. Try some widgeon or teal or pintail whistling. If there are some diving ducks in the area, try imitating a bufflehead's reedy, vibrating "b-r-r-r-r-r" call. These calls will have an even better shot if you've got some representative species in your decoy spread.

To learn how important these other sounds can be, go to a wildlife viewing area in the midst of a refuge like the Grey Lodge Management Area in central California. Ducks of every species common to the West Coast come here to rest during midday. Shut your vehicle off; open all the windows. Sit there with your eyes closed and just listen. You'll be stunned at how prevalent the whistles and grunts are over the true quacks and highballs of the mallards. Besides being educational, it's a waterfowl symphony every extreme hunter should experience at least once.

Carry a variety of calls. If it's not fully understood why ducks will come to a call, then how can we hope to understand why they prefer the sound of one model and brand of call one day and another the next? Just accept that they do and come to the blind prepared with several calls. You can keep changing until you find the one that works that day.

What does your feeding chuckle sound like? For a long time, the standard way to make the feeding chuckle of happy mallards has been to train your tongue to say "ticket, ticket, ticket" into the call as fast as you can. The result is a rapid fire "rumbling" from the call. However, the resulting sound often seems closer to the "chuckling" a flock of ducks makes when it's flying. The sound of ducks actually feeding is a little bit slower and more deliberate. Try saying, "git, git, git, git, git, git, git..." into the call and varying the energy level a bit. With practice you can perfectly mimic birds in a feeding field or oak bottom.

Blow at their butts. This advice prevents calling too much. If ducks seem to be wary of the call, only blow when they are going away from you. As soon as they turn for another look, either stop calling completely or shift immediately to soft talk like the feeding chuckle or subdued quacks.

Don't call at all. If the birds seem call-shy, try not calling at all. For most of us, that means zipping our calls into our gear bag because

our natural inclination is to try to talk them in. Instead, focus on doing whatever you can to attract distant birds to your decoys by using as much natural-appearing motion as possible.

Use the wind. Think about the times you've had to help the dog make distant retrieves on windy days. As you approach, your partner is working on another flock of birds. If you're downwind, you probably heard the calling a long way off. Upwind, you may not have been able to hear the call until you opened the door of the blind. The same holds true for the birds. Depending on which direction the birds are, compensate by calling louder or softer as necessary.

Don't call when ducks are directly overhead. Particularly if you are hunting from natural cover or in a blind without a top on it, don't call when the birds are right over the top of you. There's too much chance they'll pinpoint movement or overlooked glare inside the blind.

Never let up on geese. Unlike ducks, which often respond to start-and-stop calling, geese seem to prefer being talked to all the way to the ground. Once you start calling a flock of geese honk, squawk, growl, hum and highball at them until the guns are going off.

When calling geese, never let up on them. And keep calling even after the shooting; sometimes they'll come back!

Keep calling after you shoot at geese. Especially when you've called in three or four geese and taken one or two birds from the small flock, keep calling while you're shooting or at least start again immediately after. Many times you can bring that lone bird or pair of birds back into range to finish off a limit.

Specks are suckers. The call of the specklebelly or white-fronted goose can be one of the most difficult to learn to make, but once you've mastered it, that squeak and laugh can be deadly on Canadas, snows and blues, as well as specks.

Give them what they want. Once you've figured out what the birds seem to want to hear, don't talk yourself into trying something else. Say, for example, you're hunting from a large spread primarily for snow geese. You've got a few Canada decoys set up off to one side of the white spread and a few full-bodied mallards to the other. While you're blowing your lungs out trying to get a flock of snows to make a swing, a flock of several hundred mallards suddenly starts circling like they want in.

The natural reaction for all six hunters in the spread is to drop the goose call and start talking like a seductive hen mallard. Don't do it; at least not all of you! The snow goose yelping and yipping started the ducks working, and it will likely do a better job of finishing them than an abrupt change.

Try team calling. As waterfowl callers, we all have our strengths and weaknesses. Maybe you've got a killer highball and an awesome feeding chuckle; your best hunting partner is strong on the mid-range calls and sounds more like a lonesome hen than most hens do. So go with your strengths. Practice together at home and in the blind to create killer teamwork.

Watch where you're pointing that call. Particularly when you're calling from a pit blind or barrel blind, try to blow the call up into the open air. The acoustics of blowing from inside a covered metal container can really hurt the way a call sounds to the birds.

Try mimicking lone birds. When you're working a single and you know the bird is responding directly to you, try repeating the exact sounds the bird is making or at least mimicking the type of call it's making. If a pintail is whistling at you, try whistling back the same number of times with the same cadence.

9

An Extreme
Waterfowling Ethic

*T*he waterfowl we hunt, whether they're ducks, geese, cranes, swans or whatever, are migratory birds. Not only do they cross state boundaries in their annual movements, some of them regularly visit three countries in a single year. Even though the U.S. government has agreements with Canada and Mexico about how and when migratory birds will be hunted, setting waterfowl hunting regulations is a complex activity that will never please all the people, will seldom please most of the people and will always leave some people really upset!

The result, in the States anyway, is layers of regulation starting with the flyway framework set forth each year by the U.S. Fish & Wildlife Service. These foundations on which the states build their regulations include outside limits on season lengths, dates between which the season must fall, bag limits in general, bag limits and closures on particular species, and other special regulation mandates. These frameworks are issued in late summer based on population estimates of various species, nesting ground conditions, estimated nesting success, estimated predation and other factors. Of course, the Migratory Bird Act of 1918 also enables the federal government to set specific regulations regarding the methods and equipment that can be used to take migratory birds. Some examples of federal regulations include the ban on baiting, requirements for non-toxic shot, guns plugged to a maximum of three shells and the purchase of a federal migratory bird stamp. These are enforced nationally by both federal and state conservation agents.

On top of the general season regulations, states are often given the opportunity to offer early teal seasons or nuisance goose seasons in localized areas where Canada geese have become a health and safety problem. These each have their own special framework and mandates inside of which states must set their specific regulations, season dates and bag limits.

When the flyway frameworks are issued, the states can build their seasons and limits within those boundaries. There are often choices to be made. Sometimes the Feds will say, "You can have a 60-day season with a five-duck per day limit or a 50-day season with a six-duck per day limit." That's when the arguing starts. Merchants and marina operators and hotel owners and hunting guides obviously want the longer season. Greedy hunters who want to put more ducks in the freezer believe they'll get to shoot more by having the extra bird per day for 50 days because they'll never hunt every day of the season. The extreme waterfowlers fight for the longer season because it extends the time they can spend in the field pursuing their passion. Landowners in heavily-pressured areas might want the shorter season so the hunters aren't around to bother them for an extra week and a half.

Once that decision is made, many states look at options of splitting the season to allow maximum opportunity with locally-reared waterfowl early in the fall and the migrants at the tail-end of the season. Often, they opt for different splits in different parts of the same state.

Then there are those additional regulations the state can make and enforce on its own. Those include the sale of state waterfowl hunting stamps; gun case laws for vehicles, boats and ATVs; trespass laws; special restrictions on blind building and placement; the number of shells you can take into some heavily hunted state managed areas; and dozens of others.

Once all of this is decided, the state waterfowl regulation pamphlets are finally typeset, printed and made available to hunters. That's why in the northern tier states, where duck seasons open early, it seems that the regulation proclamations are barely out before the season. In cases of nuisance goose seasons, special regulation pamphlets have to be issued just to cover those seasons. Special tags or permits may be required as well.

If local Canada geese are causing problems, hunters often benefit from special early and late seasons to hunt the nuisance birds.

Hunting ethics are the decisions you make while hunting, of which no one but you will ever know the result.

Finally, local ordinances covering hunting and the discharge of firearms can be added to the mix. These are of special concern to waterfowl hunters whose traditional hunting areas face encroachment from expanding suburbia! Each year suburban city governments change ordinances that limit where and during what hours waterfowl hunters can hunt. Often spots that "you could always hunt on" are closed down without much fanfare.

Such is the jungle of regulations that the extreme waterfowl hunter of the 21st century faces. Knowing, understanding and living by each and every regulation placed on us by every level of government is a daunting and sometimes depressing proposition. Yet, as extreme waterfowl hunters, we understand it is the price we pay to pursue our passion. The extreme waterfowl hunter will not break the law. Instead, every single regulation must be fully understood, lived by and viewed as an added challenge that makes the successful pursuit of our game all the more rewarding.

The Ethical Extreme Waterfowler

A good working definition of "hunting ethics" is: those decisions you make while hunting, of which no one but you will ever know the result. However, it should go without saying that ethical behavior is everything above and beyond obeying the law. It is impossible to be a violator *and* a hunter with high ethics.

That's easy to say but not so easy to live by. In some cases, the law seems to come in conflict with the pursuit of high ethical standards. Say, for example, you are hunting in a managed public area which has blinds set up with a retrieving zone around a "no entry" waterfowl refuge. You shoot a goose that glides across the retrieving zone, folds up and falls stone dead within plain view but inside the refuge boundary. You know it's illegal to enter the refuge, you're not sure if it's legal to send your dog in to get the bird, but you're darn certain it is unethical to let that bird go to waste; in fact, it would likely be a violation of the wanton waste law. What do you do?

It's a pain in the butt, but the answer in this case would be to leave your blind and go find the area manager or one of the conservation officers who works the area. Alert him or her to your situation, and the agent will likely go with you or retrieve the bird for you. This is not an easy choice, but it keeps you both ethical and legal.

Another such example would be pursuing a wounded bird on open water with a motorboat. Let's say it's a bluebill that keeps diving and diving in the swells and has completely worn out your retriever. Like any owner deserving of the loyalty of an extreme retriever, you fire up the boat and race out to haul in your dog. Once he's safely on board, you look up and there's the duck sitting there at the edge of shotgun range. The motor's off and your progress from its power has ceased. You uncase the gun and load it. You pull up to dispatch the cripple and ... it's gone. You wait what seems like ten minutes, and there it pops up even farther out into the lake. You unload, case the gun, start the motor and head for the duck. It dives. You stop the motor, wait for the boat to come to a stop, uncase the gun and load it. The duck pops up, you shoot, but the bird keeps swimming. It's out of range again, so you move to the center seat and row in that direction for all you're worth, but in the waves the 'bill manages to gain ground. You unload, case the gun and fire up the motor. This time you race right up to the bird and it dives. You cut the motor, stop progress, uncase the gun and load. A minute goes by and it pops up ... back in the direction you came from and out of range. You shoot anyway, case the gun and start the motor ...

And the chase goes on and on. It would seem that the ethical choice would be to motor up to the duck with the gun loaded, put it out of its misery and add it to your bag. Except for the fact that you'd be in violation of the law, it would be. In this situation, no matter how frustrating, the chase must go on within the limits of the law until the duck is recovered or it dives and is never seen again after a reasonable amount of time and a reasonable search of the area. And the ethical extreme waterfowl hunter will count that bird in the bag limit. After all, it's as good as dead, and you killed it; that constitutes a bagged bird.

One more example may be the most common, yet that makes it no less heart-wrenching for the extreme waterfowler. A pair of canvasbacks swings wide on the marsh, then locks on your decoys. You've never bagged a bull can, and the lead bird is a beauty. Your heart pounds and maybe even skips a beat as they race to the opening in your spread which will put them right at 30 yards away. The drake drops its feet to act as air brakes and slows to settle in. You swing across his bill and squeeze the trigger just as the hen decides to speed past for one more swing. At the shot, both birds cartwheel stone dead across the water. You're a bird over your limit for cans.

The future of waterfowl hunting will be a direct reflection of the decisions we make in the blind today.

Some days, an extreme waterfowler will take a full bag like this hunter in Canada. On others, he'll be content simply to watch the birds work the decoys. Neither day is more "ethical" than the other.

The extreme waterfowl hunter feels terrible. He or she stops right there and picks up the decoys for the day, or at least cases the gun to let companions finish their limits. As soon as possible, he or she locates a conservation officer and explains what happened—then lives with the consequences.

There might be two temptations here. One is to pitch the unlucky hen into the weeds to feed the scavengers. That would be illegal and unethical. The second would be to let a partner claim that bird in his or her limit. Also illegal and unethical.

The exercise of creating and arguing about ethical dilemmas in the field could go on for eternity. Anyone who has hunted waterfowl only a few times could probably present several questionable situations based on his own experience. While the laws are there to guide us, ethical extreme waterfowl hunters must police themselves.

Avoiding Dilemmas

Obeying laws and living up to ethical standards is another part of waterfowl hunting where an ounce of prevention is definitely worth a pound of cure. And there are a number of things we can do to avoid having to make those tough decisions. All boiled down, they are simply ways to show respect for the birds, for our fellow hunters and for landowners.

Don't shoot at birds that are too far away to kill cleanly. There is no place in waterfowl hunting today for a "you can't hit 'em if you don't shoot at 'em" attitude. Skybusters have probably ruined more hunts for more people than any other cause, and they've done more to contribute to making ducks and geese spookier than any other factor. Shooting only at birds well within range will reduce the situations in which you have to deal with legal and ethical dilemmas about retrieving birds.

Work at improving your waterfowling wingshooting skills. Skybusting isn't only shooting at birds that are hopelessly beyond the range of the gun and loads you are using. Skybusting is taking shots at ranges or in situations where your wingshooting skills are not up to the task. If you're not confident you'll kill a bird stone dead when you flip the safety off, then flip it back and sit down to wait for the next one. During the off season, practice wingshooting with methods and equipment that will translate directly to the shooting you'll be doing from the blind. The better you shoot, the fewer wounded birds you'll have to deal with.

Divide up the shooting. It's illegal to "party hunt" migratory birds. And "flock shooting" is a huge frustration to extreme waterfowlers who enjoy hunting not as an exercise in filling the freezer but in testing their own hunting skills and instincts. We want to shoot our own birds! When you set up the spread or settle into the blind, decide how you'll divide up the shooting. You might have a guide or appointed hunt master call the shots on birds within range. Pairs or trios of hunters who know each other well might stake out shooting zones that dictate who will take what birds where. Hunters sitting side-by-side can agree on which birds they'll take as the flock works. Best of all is to alternate shooting between the hunters on incoming birds. Any system can work as long as the hunters agree to stick to it.

Become a master of waterfowl identification. This is easy for the extreme waterfowl hunter because of the desire to connect with waterfowl year round. Books and videotapes are important study tools, but nothing beats time actually observing birds. Being able to tell what species and sex of duck you've taken once it's in your hand is not nearly enough. The extreme waterfowl hunter learns to identify ducks and geese on the wing, at all times of the year, at all ages and under a variety of lighting conditions. He or she learns to read subtle clues like size, silhouette, wing beat speed, flight patterns and flock formations. Mistakes will happen, but you can be a great deal more confident about staying within the legal limit when you know precisely what you're shooting at!

Set "self-imposed" limits more strict than the legal limits. You can tell an extreme waterfowl hunter by the self-imposed limits he or she sets for himself or herself. Regardless of legal shooting time, few extreme waterfowl hunters will shoot until there's enough light to tell what species and sex of bird is in range. Most extreme waterfowlers are only satisfied with shooting drakes. You can tell an extreme waterfowler because he or she will be the one who shows up at the check-in station every morning with precisely one or two birds *under* the legal limit. Sometimes extreme waterfowlers will even specify on a particular morning's hunt that they'll only shoot a particular type of duck when it presents a particular type of shot. Some won't pass-shoot. Some won't jump-shoot. They don't hold it against those who do so legally and within reason, but it's not for them. The magic in setting your own limits stricter than the legal limits is that you always then allow yourself margin for error.

Part of the joy of hunting is sharing golden moments with good friends — then recalling them years later.

While it's what we do in the field that shows we are hunters, it's how we present ourselves in day-to-day life that shows non-hunters that we're the good guys!

Don't go under-gunned. Hunting is not a catch and release situation. When you slap the trigger, you've set into action a series of events which is irreversible. We owe it to our game not to let ego or braggadocio entice us into hunting with less gun than is needed for the job. Again, by selecting the proper hunting tools, you're allowing yourself margin for error.

Hunt with a well-trained dog. An extreme retriever is the waterfowl hunter's greatest conservation tool. It shows the greatest respect possible for the game to commit to the 365 days-a-year responsibilities of owning and training a retriever. Plus, a good retriever will do more than any other precaution to prevent you from worrying about ethical dilemmas of recovering the birds you shoot.

The Image We Present Of Hunting

The non-hunting public is going to view the extreme waterfowl hunter as a fanatic. By the very nature of the passion—and, yes, obsession—with which we pursue our sport, those outside of the fraternity will not be able to understand fully what it means to be an extreme waterfowl hunter. Yet because of that there is a great opportunity for us to portray the most positive things about hunting and conservation.

It should be taken as a huge compliment when word gets back to us that a landowner reports to his buddies in town, "Yeah, those guys who hunted our field yesterday sure are crazy for crane huntin'. They got there half an hour extra early to pick up every single empty shell the hunters from the week before left out in the field. They said they thought those empties would spook the birds! Can you believe it? Sure is nice they picked them up though."

Yeah, that's crazy ... crazy like foxes.

Even outside of activities directly related to hunting, it's crucial that the extreme waterfowl hunter set a good example. Because our desire is to live the waterfowl hunting lifestyle, it's likely most everyone we come in contact with will know we are hunters.

When the meter reader comes to the house, chances are it will only take one visit to tell an extreme waterfowl hunter lives there. The decoys stacked on the porch for repainting, the camouflaged boat parked behind the garage, the retriever or two or three in the kennel will all be pretty good hints.

Six months later the meter reader is at home reading the paper and recognizes your name from his route. If he's reading that you took the biology club at the local high school on a "marsh hike" to identify and count migrating birds, he is likely to think, "You know, those duck hunters are pretty good guys." On the other hand, if he reads the police report and sees the name he recognizes was cited for driving while intoxicated, then he thinks, "Yeah, those hunters are all a bunch of gun-toting drunks."

The lesson is that if you're going to wear your passion for waterfowling like a banner, then everything else you do outside of hunting is going to reflect back on all extreme waterfowlers.

Tips For A Positive Image

Don't drink and hunt. From the safety perspective alone, this one should be obvious. A drink when the guns are put away for the day and you're safely back at camp is fine. Beer cans left in the blind or in the garbage container at the public access are not.

Leave nothing but footprints. Police your blind, your hunting area and your access whether on private or public land.

Know who you are talking to. While extreme waterfowlers should take every opportunity to promote the good news about hunting in the community, know your audience when you do. If you find yourself with a group of non-hunters, talk about the teamwork between a retriever and a hunter or the benefits of wetland restoration for non-game species of birds and animals. Save the specifics of force training a stubborn dog or the details of how much more you'll get to hunt because of a new public area near town for your fellow extreme waterfowl hunters.

Dress nicely; speak well. When you're out shopping hunting leases, when you go into town for dinner after a day of hunting, when you take the Cub Scouts to the waterfowl viewing area, don't wear your favorite military camos or your "never washed" lucky hunting shirt. Dress nicely and speak with civility to the waiter or waitress. Be friendly and easygoing.

Let people know you are a hunter. When you eat at a restaurant or stop at a gas station on the way to or from a hunting trip, be sure to let the owner or manager know that their business was just patronized by a hunter who wouldn't have been there if it hadn't been for hunting!

Give back to the water-fowling. Hunters are the first and greatest conservationists. Our hunting license dollars and the special taxes we pay fund the vast majority of wildlife management and habitat restoration in this country. That's great, and we certainly should not let the non-hunting public forget it, but it's also not enough. Seek out ways to do more for the lifestyle that's done so much for you. Volunteer on local conservation boards and projects. Join Wildlife Forever, Ducks Unlimited, Waterfowl USA and any local organizations that share your views on hunting and waterfowl. The extreme waterfowler can never fully repay what he or she gets from the sport.

Giving something back to the lifestyle that's given us so much can be as simple as erecting wood duck boxes or nesting structures.

It's A Big Responsibility

Accepting the title of extreme waterfowl hunter is a big responsibility. Because you live waterfowl hunting every day of your life, every decision you make, every conversation you have, reflects back on all of the rest of us. Please do your part to make us proud to share the brand "extreme waterfowler" with you.

Index

PHOTO CREDITS

Cover onlay photo by Neal & MJ Mischler
Grady Allen: 114
Gladys Boeselager: 86
Johnnie Candle: 77, 130, 145
Dawn Charging: 4, 11, 28, 66, 72, 75, 102, 104, 112, 115, 123, 137, 138, 143, 170, 193,
Dan Dietrich: 14, 45, 116, 186
Courtesy of Federal Cartridge: 71, 83, 84
Courtesy Of Filson Company: 24
Kevin Howard: 128, 172
Mark LaBarbera: 32, 58, 59, 152, 158, 159, 160, 176, 185
Bill Miller: 6, 12, 15, 17, 22, 27, 38, 42, 48, 60, 65, 70, 79, 88, 92, 106, 109, 110, 120, 124, 125, 135, 142, 148, 174, 179, 189, 190
Dorothy Miller: 18
Courtesy Of North-East Decoy Company: 166, 169, 180
Steve Pennaz: 21
Fritz Ried: 80
Larry Sletten: 1, 8 , 31, 33, 56, 82, 98, 101
Courtesy Of Wildlife Forever: 197